This book will make you feel seen.

Copyright © 2022 by Chloë Jade

All rights reserved. No portion of this book may be reproduced, stored in a retrieval system, or transmitted, in any form, or by any means (electronic, mechanical, photocopying, recording, audiobook or otherwise) without written permission from the author.

This book is not intended as a substitute for the advice of medical and mental health professionals. The reader should regularly consult a professional in matters relating to their mental and physical health and particularly concerning any symptoms that may require diagnosis or medical attention.

No responsibility for loss caused to any individual or organisation acting on or refraining from action as a result of the material in this publication can be accepted by the publisher or author.

1st edition, 2022

A collection of 222 pieces of writing on mental health, healing, relationships, self-love + letting go.

THIS BOOK WILL MAKE YOU FEEL SEEN

This book is dedicated to

Anyone that needs to feel seen.

Let's take it one page at a time.

A note from the author

Looking back, the most healing moments in my life were simply when I felt seen. Whether that was by a therapist, friend or a stranger. Feeling seen allows us to validate our experiences and move past our pain. It's a seriously underrated part of healing. My writing is dedicated to breaking through the taboo of mental health and many other areas of life, so that we can all feel a little more connected and encouraged and a little less stuck and alienated.

I write with full awareness and acceptance that you may not resonate with every message I have to offer. However, this is the intention of my book. There is something for everyone, from all walks of life. You might not understand one piece of writing, then months later it lands open on that page and it's exactly what you needed to hear at that precise moment in time. It's not one to be read once and left on a bookshelf to collect dust. It's one that can be picked up over and over again throughout the highs and lows of your life. Highlighted. Bookmarked. Photographed. Shared. Use this book in whatever way helps you to heal, and to feel seen.

You'll find the messages in this book follow the themes of acknowledging your pain, feeling your feelings, letting go of the things holding you back and curating healthier relationships, including the one you have with yourself. This book is a safe space to feel all of that confusing heaviness, without all of the overthinking, guilt and suppression that many of us fall victim to.

One last note, I am the writer behind @intuitivejournals on Instagram and TikTok. If you do use social media, feel free to get in touch, you have my full permission to share pages of my book and tag me. I love to see the places and people my writing has reached. I think it's incredible how someone you've never met can make you feel so seen. There's a handful of writers that have done that for me over the years and my heart is so full knowing I get to be that person for others now. So truly, thank you for being here, thank you for picking up this book to read. I may not be there with you in person but I aim to be through the words on these pages. A lot of love has gone into this one. I'm so glad it found its way to you.

I might not understand every struggle you've been through. Or every secret you hold. I may not understand the waves of emotions or numbness you experience.

But I do see you.

I recognise the pain you go through. I recognise how lonely you feel on your healing journey. I know how it feels to wish you could switch it off and run away from it all.

I can see that you've made it through all of your worst days so far. I can see all of the emotions you keep bottled up that sometimes come flooding over the edges when somebody asks if you're okay. I can see that despite everything, you still try to be a better person.

I see you for all of that.

I know it doesn't always feel like it but you truly have made an impact on the world. Some people's faces light up when they see you. Some of your birthday cards and handwritten notes are tucked away in a drawer somewhere. That stranger was having a bad day and your smile turned it around. Someone still uses that gift you gave them 3 years ago. You're the reason somebody has to hold in their laugh at the most inconvenient moment when they remember something funny you did a long time ago. You make people feel safe. You make people feel loved.

The world feels lighter with you in it.

So thank you, thank you for being here. Thank you for making this world a better place to be. Thank you for all you've done.

Can I tell you something, which you may be resistant to hear but truly need to understand if you're ever to be free from the constraints of your own mind?

You don't have to earn love. Love is not a currency. Love is a birthright. You do not have to struggle for love. You do not have to prove you are worthy of love. You are not hard to love. Other people's inability to love you in a healthy way does not mean you are unworthy of love. Your own inability to love yourself does not mean you are unworthy of love. Your inability to love others does not mean they are unworthy of love.

And you may ask, well what about bad people, do they deserve to be loved? Perhaps, if they grew up in a home and society full of unconditional love instead of fear and hate, maybe they would not project the pain and experiences they had onto others. Does it excuse their behaviour? No. But it is a reminder to you that you are not inherently unworthy of love because you've mirrored all you've ever known.

Actually, you did deserve better.

You did deserve to feel unconditionally loved and supported as a child. You did deserve to be comforted on your worst days. You did deserve to have your talents and dreams recognised. You did deserve to be cheered on. You did deserve to be taught how to navigate your big emotions with gentleness and understanding instead of neglect and anger. You did deserve love even through your awkward, stubborn, angry teenager phases. You did deserve to be forgiven for all the mistakes you made and learned from. You did deserve to be acknowledged for trying your best.

And do you know what?

You still do. You still deserve all of that compassion, love and acceptance. If no one was around to give it to you, I am so sorry, I know it hurts. And I know you shouldn't have to, but it's time to learn how to give it to yourself.

Have you ever cried yourself to sleep? Cried softly into a pillow so you couldn't be heard? Have you mastered the art of tears rolling down your cheeks without making a sound? Because you don't want to be a burden? You don't want others to see your inner world? Do you think if you let them in, you'll be abandoned and rejected more than you already have?

Is that you? Can I tell you something which you might find hard to believe, but I know to be true?

You are not a burden. You are not too much. You are not broken. You are not annoying. You don't cry too loud and you're not dramatic. I am so sorry you've been made to feel like you have to hide away.

You deserve to be held. You deserve to be listened to. You deserve to ugly cry, for as many days as you need to. That's a lot of pain you're holding and it's okay to let it all out. It doesn't serve you anymore. Let it all out, my love. Let it all out.

Healing is hard.

There's no way about it. 'Oh you just need to go to therapy for a few weeks and you'll be fine.' 'Oh you'll get over it one day, it's in the past, it doesn't matter now.' 'Just change the way you think!'

No, it probably won't all go away in a few weeks of therapy and actually, I do think it matters now.

If your past is distracting you from being present, no matter how small you perceive your experiences to be, you have to look into that. You don't have to dwell on it, but you do need to acknowledge it.

Healing is hard. But do you know what's harder? Living in fear. Gaslighting yourself. Pretending that you're not hurt and you don't struggle to process painful emotions. Having to use all of your energy to consistently push the past deep down inside of you instead of letting it come to the surface. In the long run, avoiding healing is much harder than doing the inner work to heal.

You can read as many self-help books as you want, and you can learn all of the psychology hacks and spiritual healing techniques but at the end of the day if you're not feeling your feelings you're always going to be faced with the same issues. Your emotions are messengers. They will keep getting louder and louder until you slow down and listen.

You might think pushing away your emotions works but avoidance turns into anger. Resentment. Bitterness. Self-hatred. Numbness. Addictions. Projections. Outbursts. Mood swings. Exhaustion. You can run and run all you want but those feelings will turn into enemies and slowly ruin your chance at experiencing a beautiful life if you refuse to learn how to befriend them.

Wow, being a teenager is hard right?

I just remember, being treated like a child yet everyone expected me to act like an adult. But no one ever taught me how to be an adult. I was told, "oh wait until you're my age, then you'll know how hard life is, and then you'll know what being tired means."

They could not have been further from the truth.

If you're a teenager reading this, I just want you to know, many of the people you're expected to look up to are just unhealed children in adult bodies. They don't have it all figured out either. Especially if they're invalidating your struggles. Your feelings are valid.

And if you're an adult reading this, let's start healing our inner teen. Let's start listening to what teenagers need from us instead of putting them down. Don't you remember how dreadfully adults treated you? Don't be that adult. Be the adult you needed in your life as a teen.

Do you feel safe in this relationship? Do you feel safe to be yourself? Do you feel safe expressing your needs?

Have you ever slowed down to consider these things?

We can get so wrapped up in hoping that the other person likes being around us, that we forget to ask ourselves if we like being around them. You deserve to be around people that allow you to be vulnerable. People that still love you when you feel like a mess. You shouldn't have to hide away your interests, true personality or feelings to keep other people happy. You're allowed to take up space and you're allowed to be authentic. You're allowed to change your perspectives and path without feeling the need to constantly justify it to other people.

Surround yourself with people that make you feel safe to be who you are, to grow and evolve, to have big feelings and to make mistakes.

I know you run those same mistakes back and forth in your mind but if you forgive yourself and let them go, you'll free up so much emotional and mental energy.

You're allowed to make mistakes. Not just one, but hundreds of them. The most important thing is that you learn from them, you take the lesson and move forward.

Life is one big game of trial and error and mistakes are what allow us to grow and redirect us to the right path.

When people say 'you need to push yourself out of your comfort zone' but you're someone that's from a broken home, or traumatic childhood, I think it might be safe to dismiss that advice. Even just for a short while.

If you're still in survival mode, I think the only thing you need to do 'to push yourself outside of your comfort zone' is to embrace the discomfort that comes with creating a comfort zone. Because you might not even have a place, physically or metaphorically speaking, where you feel safe and comfortable. And creating a life of peace and stability can feel uncomfortable when you're not used to that.

So maybe, even just for this chapter of your journey, you can let go of the need to achieve more, and work on embracing the feeling of calm instead of chaos.

You're not only allowed to have big feelings, you're also allowed to express them.

It's quite bizarre really that we're expected to go around blank-faced all of the time when as far as we know, we're the only species on Earth to have been given such a wide spectrum of complex emotions.

When we're born, our first communication with the world is an ear-piercing cry. But, it's the most beautiful sound in the world, right? Knowing the baby has been born healthy enough to make such a sound. Then the baby continues to cry whenever it needs something. It's a survival instinct. A cry for help. It's quite literally life-saving.

Yet now, we feel so much shame for the same survival instinct. Just because we can intellectualise our feelings, it doesn't mean we need to avoid expressing them.

All of this is to say, it's okay to cry.

I hope you know that even on the days you feel like you've failed, you're allowed to be proud of yourself.

Because it's not about the destination at the end of the day. If you want to, I'm sure you can still get there by trying another way, or maybe you'll be redirected to something even greater, something way more aligned.

It's about the journey you took, and all that you learned about yourself on that journey. It's the fact you picked yourself off of the floor and kept trying.

Please don't be disappointed in yourself if the end result wasn't what you hoped. It's okay to feel sad about it but beating yourself up won't move you any closer to your goals. You're allowed to be proud of yourself just for trying. Just for making it through another tough road.

But this isn't the end. You can try again. You can try a thousand more times if you need to. Just don't give up on yourself. Don't give up on your dreams.

Maybe, just for this chapter of your life, you don't need another relationship. Maybe the relationship you really need is the one you've been neglecting the most; the one you have with yourself.

Have you ever shown yourself the same care, compassion and love that you've shown to others? Have you ever asked yourself what you need from yourself? Have you ever really appreciated yourself, all that you do, all that you have done?

Leaning away from relationships outside of ourselves for a little while can strengthen them in the long run. The healthier the relationship you have with yourself, the healthier the relationships you can form outside of yourself.

Stop pouring so much into others, and start pouring back into yourself.

You deserve to feel seen.

You deserve to have your voice heard.

You deserve to be listened to.

You deserve to feel appreciated.

You deserve to feel safe.

You deserve to take up space.

You deserve to feel at home within your body.

You deserve to be surrounded by good people.

You deserve good experiences.

You deserve to eat good food.

You deserve to have a warm home.

You deserve to find joy every day.

You are a light in this world.

Never forget that.

You may not realise it but you inspire others by simply being you. Your energy is a source of comfort. Your gentleness and compassion is a precious virtue in this harsh world.

I hope you know how special and loved you are, especially on the days you feel low. I hope the world reciprocates all of that gentle loving energy back to you. You deserve to experience all the good the world has to offer. Thank you for being you.

To all the people that have been moved from place to place or had a rocky home life, it's okay if you don't feel a true sense of home yet.

You might have tried to find the comfort and safety of 'home' within others, and that might have caused more damage in the long run. Especially if for whatever reason you had to go your separate ways. It is incredibly painful to feel lost again after feeling at home for a while.

Can I offer you a new solution? Could you maybe find a feeling of home within yourself, within your own body and mind, so that you can take it with you wherever you go? A sort of inner peace and stability that will never leave you.

I'm not sure how that would look for you, but it's saved me from desperately seeking home within others. And it's helped me to heal a vast feeling of emptiness that I didn't realise I was carrying around for so long.

27

Do you really want to disappear? Or, if you are honest with yourself, do you just want to be found?

Because I'm guessing if you picked up this book, you need someone to see and validate all of the painful emotions and intrusive thoughts you're struggling with.

You're exhausted and you want somebody to tell you to rest. You feel unloved and you want somebody to love you unconditionally. You feel abandoned and you want someone to promise you that they'll never leave. You feel like a failure, but you just want someone to be proud of you.

So allow me.

Please get some rest. I love you unconditionally. Maybe I can't be there for you in person, but my words will be with you forever. I am so proud of you. Regardless of how you feel right now, you are always loved. Because I love you. You deserve good things in life.

If you go around defining yourself by other people's ideas of success then you will never feel successful.

If you go around defining yourself by other people's ideas of intelligence then you will never feel intelligent.

If you go around defining yourself by other people's ideas of kindness then you will never feel kind enough.

If you go around defining yourself by other people's ideas of happiness then you will never feel happy.

Why? Because every single person, every culture, every country, every workplace, and every school, defines these things in a different way.

And you cannot be all of them, all at once. They are all mutually exclusive.

You get to decide. You don't have to define yourself based on what you've been told your whole life.

On your way to where you want to be, you don't have to stop yourself from experiencing joy. You do not have to deprive yourself of all the good things life has to offer to 'deserve' to achieve your goals.

It's okay to slow down for 10 minutes and really enjoy your cup of coffee or tea. It's okay to watch your favourite comfort movie again. It's fine to stop and watch the sunset for a moment instead of rushing home.

No matter how big the gap between where you are now and where you want to be, filling the space in between with little moments of joy and gratitude isn't going to derail your success.

It's okay to slow down and it's okay to rest. This time now is just as important as any other moment in time.

Let go of the guilt of simply being alive.

This is your sign to stop waiting for other people to give you permission and validation to make that change or go for that dream life that's been on your mind.

Some people will never understand your vision for your life and that's okay. I'm sure there have been many times when you didn't understand why other people made a certain life choice.

Going around trying to convince other people to give you the go-ahead is going to drain your energy, energy which you can use to achieve whatever it is you want to do. Trust yourself. Trust your intuition.

a letter to anyone feeling 'behind in life'

It's actually impossible to be behind when you're on your own path. You can't be a minute ahead or a minute late. You're right on time.

Think about the trees. They all grow differently, at their own rate, in different environments. If every tree grew at the exact same time and looked identical, it would be a very dull and monotonous world to live in.

There's beauty in diversity. I think some of the most interesting people are the ones that follow their own timeline. Breaking tradition. Figuring out life slowly. Achieving goals later in life than the norm.

It's really no one else's business what you choose to do with your life. We all end up dying in the end anyway. You have no one to live life for but yourself. Do what's best for you. And take your time with it.

You say 'I'm just tired' and they just think you haven't been sleeping well.

But there are so many different types of tiredness.

Emotionally tired. Physically tired. Socially tired. Spiritually tired. Empty tired. Overworked tired. I don't have much left to give tired. Misunderstood tired. Unseen tired. Disconnected tired. I miss them tired. I feel lost tired. Those deadlines are filling me with anxiety tired. Everyone expects so much of me tired.

So I get it.

You're just tired of being tired.

There will be chapters of your life where you feel inspired to hustle, to never stop working. To do everything in your power to be as productive as possible.

There will also be chapters of your life where you feel the need to do nothing other than simply exist. To rest and just allow yourself to recharge.

You may come to the realisation that too much of the former leads to burnout and too much of the latter leads to feeling unfulfilled. And many influencers and motivational speakers only preach one or the other. There feels like pressure to choose.

You can have a balance though. You can work hard towards your goals and take regular breaks. You can create a better future whilst finding peace in the present. Be mindful of the way an 'all or nothing' mindset can damage your psyche.

This won't be a message that resonates with everyone, but if your heartbreak feels traumatic, it might not be about them. It might be that you have some abandonment wounds from your childhood finally being uncovered.

It's normal to feel an enormous amount of pain after a separation, but feeling like you'll never be able to survive without them, is usually a sign that there's something deeper inside of you that needs healing.

My body was in such a state of shock after a breakup that I couldn't eat or sleep for weeks. I was obsessed with needing them back. It felt like life or death. Even though I knew in my heart that they weren't right for me. I wish someone had told me, it wasn't about them. They were just a trigger for some much-needed self-discovery and a return to self-love.

The phrase 'other people can't love you unless you love yourself' is incredibly damaging and untrue.

I have loved many people that absolutely despise themselves. I have loved them unconditionally whilst they battle an internal war in their minds. I would never dream of telling someone in my life that they're unlovable because they are unable to see their own worth. What a ridiculous idea.

However, I can understand the phrase from a point of view that it's harder to accept acts of love if you don't love yourself. It's harder to accept compliments, gifts, acts of service, physical intimacy and quality time. But just because you're personally struggling with self-love, it doesn't mean other people also find it hard to love you.

Self-love takes time and you deserve to be surrounded by people that can support you and inspire you throughout that healing journey.

I know when you've been hurt over and over again that it feels easy to say you'll never trust anyone again. You'll never open yourself up to love ever again.

I've been there, I've been you. It hurts like hell.

But you do deserve to allow yourself to be loved by others. One day your heart will heal and you will trust yourself enough to choose relationships that feel healthy, loyal and supportive to you.

Even if you've spent your whole life being surrounded by untrustworthy, hurtful people, that's still only a tiny proportion of the population of the world. Good people do exist and they will love you whole-heartedly. They will stay by you even when things get hard.

Don't shut yourself out from the fear of pain, because the feeling of being unconditionally loved will far surpass that fear.

If you're somebody that feels like your pain and problems aren't enough to receive recognition, I'm here to affirm to you that they are.

Especially if you've grown up in a household where someone had a physical / mental illness, trauma, addiction, or period of grief that meant they received the most attention.

Just because others neglect to see that you're struggling, doesn't mean that your feelings are automatically invalid.

You wouldn't leave a broken leg untreated because other people are suffering from asthma. There is room for you too. There is space for your feelings and experiences to be heard too. You don't have to be the one to keep it all together all of the time.

You deserve to be in a work environment that values you as a human being instead of expecting you to be an emotionless machine. You're allowed to set boundaries at work, with people, with hours and with the way you're treated. And if those boundaries are disrespected, you're allowed to leave.

I know you're thinking, well I need the money or 'what if something else doesn't come up?'

There will always be other jobs. There will always be other sources of income. Even if you have to search for a job while putting up with your current job. I know it's tough and you shouldn't have to do that to survive, but don't feel like you're obliged to stay. You don't owe a person or company anything. You have autonomy, they do not own you. You deserve to be respected. You don't have to destroy yourself mentally and physically for anyone, especially not for a job that would replace you if you disappeared tomorrow. This life is yours to live.

It doesn't matter how much you love someone, or how much they claim to love you, you don't have to stay in a relationship that isn't serving you.

If you feel controlled, suffocated, like you have to make changes or sacrifices that take away your peace and happiness, love isn't enough of a reason to stay.

Relationships can feel challenging at times, but love shouldn't feel hard. You shouldn't feel drained all of the time. You shouldn't have to beg for your needs to be met. You should only need to communicate that they've hurt you once. You shouldn't have to keep reminding them of that because they refuse to take accountability for their actions. You shouldn't feel scared or alone. You're allowed to walk away, even if every ounce of your being loves that person. Sometimes the healthiest thing you can do is love someone from a distance, and pour all of that excess love back into yourself.

Struggling to sleep at night, or having nightmares and vivid dreams, then being expected to carry on with your day as normal in the morning is extremely difficult.

You're exhausted yet your performance is expected to be the same as someone that got 8 or 9 hours of consistent sleep all week.

I know not many people understand the exhaustion and fragility you feel. But you do, and that's reason enough to be gentle with yourself. Stop putting pressure on yourself to pour out the same amount of energy and work as someone that has a healthy sleep schedule.

The same applies if you're someone that has those traumatic dreams that wake you up in cold sweats and repeat on loop in your mind all day.

Give yourself grace as you navigate life without having one of your basic survival needs met.

41

Have you decided that you don't fit into a box? The labels that society has laid out for you don't quite fit your description of you?

What they don't tell you is when you realise you don't fit into a box, there's an overwhelmingly vast amount of space outside the box. So now you feel lost because you're just this small human in a big world of endless possibilities.

Yet you're still stuck in a world that loves to put labels on everything. Like a social shortcut. So we can quickly make assumptions about people rather than taking the time to truly get to know them as an individual that's experienced life in a million different ways to us.

You no longer have the shortcut labels to describe yourself to others. So then, you feel like you're a nobody. But really, you're just somebody that can't pick a few defining labels to describe yourself. Because you know, in your heart, that you are so much more than that. And you don't want other people to perceive you based on a few words alone. You want to truly feel seen and understood. That's completely valid.

So maybe you can let go of the need to try and explain yourself to others. Let go of the need to justify your lack of labels and accept that you are simply, you. The people that are meant to be in your life, will be curious to get to know you as this interesting, indescribable, multifaceted being. They're not going to care about the superficial categories others put you under.

You're not just (insert age), (insert job title), (insert background), (insert relation), (insert health issues), (insert hobby) and (insert defining personality trait).

You're actually (insert hundreds of different possibilities).

Just because all that you've been through has gone unseen and misunderstood by others doesn't mean you need to dismiss yourself and your feelings in the same way. No one can comprehend the horrors you've been through because they're not you. You've been through so much, without proper care and time to rest and yet you still put all of this pressure on yourself to achieve the same as someone that hasn't lived even a day of your life.

Your time of healing, productivity and joy will come. Your spark will come back. You will find people that understand you and love you as you are. But in the meantime, please take good care of yourself. Please be more gentle with yourself. Speak to yourself with the same love and patience you would your best friend.

In a world that expects you to put on a happy face everyday, I think it's incredibly brave of you to be vulnerable with your emotions. I hope you realise by doing so you're breaking through generations of trauma and limiting beliefs, and that is an incredibly difficult thing to do. You're making the world a safer place to be in. When you break through the taboo of emotions and mental health, you're leading the way for others to do the same. Countless lives have been saved just from the people that are brave enough to speak up about the things we've been told to be silent about. It doesn't make you weak at all. There's so much strength in vulnerability and I hope you can recognise that in yourself.

It's not your responsibility to use your emotional intelligence to decipher people that are emotionally immature. Your emotional intelligence is for you to understand and communicate your own needs and emotions. It's not for you to intellectualise and guess someone else's feelings from the weight of their footsteps, the loudness of their sighs or their silent treatment. It is their responsibility as an adult to have the self-awareness and maturity to communicate their emotions through language. If they are unable to do that, especially after you have asked, it is more than okay to distance yourself to protect your own peace.

There's nothing wrong with you if you didn't find therapy helpful. You may have had the loveliest therapist, but what you might not have been told is not every therapist is a great match for every person.

Sometimes you just need to find one that offers a different type of practice, or has more understanding of your pain. There's therapists that intellectualise pain, and there's others that empathise with pain. Some are practising from textbooks, others are practising from life experiences. Some a mixture of both. Different approaches work for different people.

One therapist cannot heal every person in the world, so no, you're not broken if it didn't work for you. In the same way it's okay to let relationships go, it's okay to let go of a therapist that doesn't align with you. As long as you are open and willing to help yourself, the problem isn't you, the problem is finding the right person, or group of specialised people that can truly help to support you and meet your needs.

If self-love feels out of reach for you, recognise that it's not a feeling you seek but the relationship you practise having with yourself. You don't have to stand naked in the mirror and think you're the most beautiful person on the earth like many self-proclaimed spiritual gurus teach. It's being able to forgive yourself and learn from your mistakes. It's being able to dry your tears and pick yourself up on the bad days. It's making sure you're meeting your basic needs. It's accepting that you do have insecurities, and that's okay. You can have insecurities and still love yourself. You can have any emotion and still love yourself. It's being able to notice your negative thoughts and consistently trying to speak kinder things to yourself. It's being able to set boundaries and live by your values. It's learning to trust yourself and your inner wisdom to do what's best for you. Practising self-compassion, self-discipline, self-respect and self acceptance is self-love. Self-love isn't limited to how you view your physical appearance or how you compare to others. It's much deeper and much more soulful than that.

I truly believe the most beautiful people in the world are the ones that have been through hell, yet still try to make heaven a place on Earth. Those people that have repeatedly had their hearts broken but still show more empathy, kindness and humanity than the average person. They really deserve a break, and they deserve more credit. They're often the same people that are most forgotten about. They ask everyone else how they are but rarely does anyone reciprocate the question.

So if you are that person, please give yourself the same love and kindness you pour into others. And if you know someone in your life like this, don't forget to thank them and check-in with them too. They deserve to feel seen.

If you've been told that your mental illness isn't real because 'we never used to have any of this back in our day,' this one's for you.

It's not that mental illness didn't exist, it's that there was a severe lack of awareness and taboo surrounding it.

The older generations have been carrying around more pain and bottled up emotions than we can comprehend. They were never given the opportunity to speak about mental health issues which makes you realise why they're so angry and project all of their pain onto other people. They were told to just get on with life.

PTSD wasn't even a household term until the 1980s. Just 40 years ago from the date I am writing this. Can you imagine leaving your loved ones, battling in a war and seeing the most inhumane acts of horror and then being expected to come back to life and act as normal?

There are many studies now that say trauma can be passed down generations. You're not just struggling with your own experiences, you're also carrying the weight of the unhealed wounds of the generations before you.

Our generation is healing to break these cycles. We don't have to save the whole world but by learning how to become more emotionally intelligent, more accepting, more compassionate, we are bringing a new level of peace to this planet.

By acknowledging what older generations could not, you are participating in a healing butterfly effect.

Social anxiety isn't shyness, it's a feeling of a lack of safety in social situations. It's repeating the same simple phrases over and over again so you don't mess up speaking to a stranger. It's feeling like all eyes are on you, every laugh is directed towards you. It's feeling like you're not welcome anywhere and you shouldn't take up space. It's fearing you're too quiet or too loud, you're speaking too much or not enough. It's fearing what people might say or do to you. Constantly checking your surroundings for danger. It's being exhausted simply from being perceived by people you don't even care about. It's avoiding leaving the house, avoiding phone calls, shaking at the thought of having to speak in front of others, even just via voice notes.

All of this comes down to feeling unsafe. If you can create feelings of safety within yourself, it becomes easier to show up in the world. I can tell you all day that it doesn't matter what others think about you, but it won't help if you've grown up around people that broke your trust. You deserve to feel safe.

There's really no soulful way for me to say this. Some people are just downright rude. And it can be your own family and friends that give you the biggest insecurities.

I don't think I could ever understand the need to point out negative things about another person's appearance. Or things they cannot change. It's just cruel. It creates unnecessary pain.

You're not too sensitive, dramatic or 'can't take a joke' because other people are unnecessarily hurtful towards you.

When you love someone, you want the best for them. That means lifting them up instead of risking making them feel small, ugly, stupid or unworthy.

Other people projecting their own judgements, pain and insecurities onto you is not an act of love, and it does not determine your worth.

If you're someone that can feel on top of the world one day and then completely hopeless the next, your feelings are still valid. Feeling the depths of the dark can make the light feel ten times brighter.

Healing isn't linear and it's very human to experience a wide range of emotions day-to-day. On those days when you do feel low, it doesn't mean all of the progress you've made has been taken away.

It may feel confusing but don't you feel alive compared to the numbness you used to feel? I know if I had a choice I'd take the rollercoaster of emotions over the feeling of complete emptiness any day.

Dear people pleasers,

You have to do what's best for <u>you</u>.

You have to do what's best for <u>you</u>.

You have to do what's best for <u>you</u>.

You have to do what's best for <u>you</u>.

You have to do what's best for <u>you</u>.

You have to do what's best for <u>you</u>.

You have to do what's best for <u>you</u>.

You have to do what's best for <u>you</u>.

You have to do what's best for <u>you</u>.

You have to do what's best for <u>you</u>.

You have to do what's best for <u>you</u>.

You have to do what's best for <u>you</u>.

You have to do what's best for <u>you</u>.

You have to do what's best for <u>you</u>.

Keep reading that until it really sinks in.

You've experienced life in thousands of different ways, big and small, to others. No one has had the exact sequence of life experiences, emotions and thoughts as you. So there's really no use in going around wasting your energy comparing yourself to others in a negative way. You are not them and they are not you and that's what makes life incredibly beautiful. If everyone looked identical and had the exact same experiences, we'd all be robots. There would be no diversity. Life would be extremely boring. The differences between all of us, is what makes this world so interesting and unique. Just because you don't live up to society's current beauty standards or ever-changing definition of success, does not make you any less beautiful, intelligent or interesting. There are people in this world that will find you to be the most fascinating person they have ever laid eyes on and they will love everything about you. You may even already have some silent admirers. Different is good. Different is human. Different is beautiful.

Life after a heartbreak, trauma or a period of deep healing can be very difficult to navigate. You have been through such a depth of different emotions and perspective shifts. Maybe even survival mode. And you've found it hard to relate to others whilst they go on about their regular day. How do you even make small talk when all you think about is how heavy your heart feels or the most horrific event repeating in your head?

Then when you have come out of the other end of it all, you feel exhausted and fragile. It's hard to sort of slot yourself back into regular life. You feel like a completely new version of you, and not everyone understands that. Not everyone understands that you haven't been working on regular life goals. But the people that have had to take time out to heal, will get you. So don't worry if you feel misunderstood now. You will likely cross paths with many people that do understand what you've been through.

This society doesn't give us much space to process anger and rage in a healthy way. So if you've had to bottle all of that up, I really do feel for you.

It's one of the most explosive emotions, and not having a safe space to release it is really unfair.

Especially when others have released their emotional poison onto you, and scarred you emotionally or physically for life.

It's not fair and there's no way around that. It wasn't fair then and it's not fair now. Don't let anyone tell you it just is what it is and to suck it up and move on. You have every right to be angry and feel injustice.

I hope you can find a healthy outlet. Revenge is never the answer. It only leads to more pain and suffering.

Obsession. Checking your notifications every minute. Checking their profile every hour. Typing out those paragraphs in your notes app. Worrying about who they're with or what they're doing. Whether they'll ever come back to you.

Listen, you did deserve closure. And I'm sorry if you never got that. But more so, you deserve to release this person energetically so you can move on with your life.

Getting them back isn't going to bring you peace because you'll be constantly worrying if they'll hurt you again. Redirect all of that attention back into yourself and watch your life transform.

Even if you truly feel you're meant to be together one day, you'll want to be the most healed and happy version of you so you don't go repeating the same cycles.

No person is worth staying up all night crying and questioning your worth for. I can promise you that.

Don't forget, sometimes we're the problem. Sometimes we're the one trying to have control over people and situations that we need to let go of. Sometimes we're the one that pushes people away. Sometimes we project our pain and insecurities onto others. Sometimes we're the ones that act irrationally from a place of jealousy. Sometimes we're the one that needs to check our attitude. Sometimes we're the ones that aren't communicating in a healthy way. The point of this isn't to start beating ourselves up for the mistakes we've made. But understanding that healing doesn't make us superior to others. Sometimes we need to be brutally honest with ourselves about how we're showing up in the world and make some significant changes. Healing isn't just about acknowledging how others hurt us, it's also acknowledging how we hurt others and ourselves. How we victimise ourselves. Leaving behaviours unchecked can mean we're our own biggest pain point.

Communication is great but it only works when all of the people involved are committed to understanding one another. You can speak your truth all day long but not hear a word the other person is saying and vice versa. You don't have to agree with them but for healthy communication to work you do need to be able to hold space and really listen to their point of view.

You haven't failed then, if you communicated and nothing changed. Some people are so stuck in their own dogmatic ways of thinking, they don't have the mental capacity to see things from any other perspective. Sometimes taking a step back from a person or conversation after nothing has changed, is a form of communication in itself.

Hurting and healing can be really messy. Emotionally and literally speaking. It can be unwashed clothes scattered around your room. Dirty dishes piled sky high. Greasy hair and unbrushed teeth. It can be crying hysterically until your eyelids puff up. Or zoning out for hours on end. Unanswered text messages. Not eating or eating too much. Not sleeping or sleeping too much. Never leaving the house or never going home.

Many people talk about mental health until it comes down to hygiene. Then you're shamed for not taking better care of yourself. Your brain is already making that an impossible task then people make it harder by adding embarrassment and taboo to the mix.

There's no shame in the messy side of it all. You'll clean it all up one day. And if it feels too overwhelming right now, start with the tiniest thing. Just throw one piece of rubbish away. Brush your teeth for 10 seconds. Put on a fresh pair of underwear. Then be proud of yourself for that. Be proud of all the progress you make.

New beginnings and big changes always come with this assumption that you'll be over the moon with excitement and joy. It's okay if you're nervous, anxious, exhausted, overwhelmed or feeling a whole mix of emotions. You're shedding old layers and letting go, sometimes you might even need to grieve the past before you can feel fully present in this new chapter. It's a lot for your brain and body to process. It's going to take a few weeks for your nervous system to settle down. Be gentle with yourself as you navigate this change.

You can do it. You can learn to love yourself. You can create a better life for yourself. You can meet new people and form healthier relationships. You can change your career. You can move to that place. You can heal from your past. You can start a new hobby. You can put yourself out there. You can. If every part of you wants something, don't let people tell you that you can't. Don't listen to that voice inside of your head that tells you that you can't. Don't be angry at it, it's just trying to keep you safe from the unknown.

Calmly respond to that voice with 'actually I can.'

THIS BOOK WILL MAKE YOU FEEL SEEN

If you're on a journey to the other side of the world and all you have is a small rucksack of belongings and an old beaten up boat, why are you comparing yourself to someone that has a private jet and a personal assistant? You might think you're on the exact same journey as someone else because you have the same destination, but if you don't have as much privilege or support, please be kinder to yourself. Please give yourself more credit. You're trying not to sink whilst some people are being lifted into the air with a cocktail in their hand. Some people don't have the trauma, or financial issues, or health issues that you've had to suffer through. Some people have 20 people cheering them on for doing the bare minimum whereas you might just have me cheering you on through these words on a page. Look to people that have done incredible things that have been through similar struggles to you, not the people that already had it all laid out for them. They're not bad people, but there is no use comparing yourself to them.

I know you want to save the world. I know you want to help everyone heal. But that's not your responsibility. Your only responsibility is to heal yourself. When you heal yourself you are indirectly healing others. You start showing up in a more open and compassionate way. You stop enabling people's toxic behaviours due to the boundaries you now hold up high. You're keeping people accountable without hijacking their own healing journey. You cannot help someone that does not want to be helped. You cannot do the healing or feel the pain for them. You cannot teach them lessons they need to learn for themselves. Be the example, transform yourself and watch how others follow in your footsteps.

Connection isn't enough. Communication isn't enough. Compatibility isn't enough. Chemistry isn't enough. You need a healthy balance of all of these. You need mutual respect. You need a willingness to learn and grow together. You need understanding and compassion. There's nothing wrong with you if you feel like you've failed to make a relationship work. It's a two way street that requires a lot of love, maturity, self-awareness and empathy. Relationships can be a lot easier with somebody that's aligned with your values. Somebody that can reciprocate the energy and work you put in. You don't have to stay with someone that drains you and refuses to take accountability for their half of the relationship.

Some people will come into your life at exactly the right time, even for just a brief moment, and bring you the biggest sigh of relief. To just know that a person like that exists is a huge weight off of your shoulders. The kind of people whose energy and perspective on life restores your faith in humanity. The kind of people that light up your day just from being around. You love them for them, exactly as they are. You want to hold onto them forever but you know, some people are just a chapter in your story, and you're grateful to have met them nonetheless. A piece of that person will forever live on in your heart and mind and you know you'll never forget them.

You are that person to somebody.

I know you settle for less than you deserve because you're afraid of being alone. You're afraid of the heartbreak and the healing. The space in between. But I promise you, you can let go. You can realise your worth. Nothing is lonelier than losing yourself in a relationship, constantly trying to make the other person happy.

You can use the alone time to feel fulfilled, to find yourself outside of relationships. And it will be hard some days but ultimately the most beautiful journey you'll ever take. You come out of the end feeling secure and truly comprehending your value. Then you can choose relationships that light you up inside instead of leaving you feeling empty and like an afterthought.

You deserve to be chosen. Over and over again.

On Monday you feel tired and like giving up.

Then on Tuesday you feel a glimpse of hope.

Wednesday, you feel pretty excited.

On Thursday you're starting to feel like yourself again.

Friday, you cry yourself to sleep.

Then on Saturday you feel anxiety build in your chest.

On Sunday, you feel at peace with yourself.

Do you know what this is called?

It's called healing. It's called being a human. Every single feeling, from Monday through to Sunday, is completely valid. You're allowed to feel the ups and downs of life. One emotion does not take validity away from the other.

Slammed doors. Silent treatment. Change in tone of voice. Shouting, swearing and screaming. Somebody coming too close. Loud sighs. Heavy footsteps. Unanswered texts. Feeling watched. Communal spaces. Spilling a drink. Drunk stumbling. The smell of alcohol. Empty eye contact. Sudden movement. Unpredictability. Aggression. The calm before the storm.

If any of these things bring up a lot of heavy emotions for you, these are your triggers. There may be many more.

Remind your inner child or past self that they're safe now. You've got them. You see them. You're here for them. You'll take them to a safer space.

It's not your fault.

No really, I mean that.

It's not your fault if you were neglected.
It's not your fault if you were abandoned.
It's not your fault if you were cheated on.
It's not your fault if you were abused.
It's not your fault if you were lied to.

It's not your fault if you were failed by the people that were meant to support, love and protect you as a child. That was their job. To be a responsible adult. Your job was just to be a child.

It's not your fault if a person could not be loyal or respectful towards the commitment you had agreed upon. They had the choice to love you or leave you. There was never meant to be a third option where they hurt you and gaslight you into thinking that is love.

Stop torturing yourself by asking what you did to deserve that. You didn't do anything wrong. You didn't deserve that. There is no justification for any of those things. You are not to blame for other peoples' actions. Adults are 100% responsible for their behaviours and how they treat other people. They are 100% responsible for treating people with a basic level of respect or leaving if they cannot provide that. It's not your fault.

I'm sorry you were born into the world with a pure heart and a lot of love to give and you have been broken over and over again.

And thank you, thank you for all of the times you got backup and kept going. All of the times you were kind to the world when it was not so kind to you.

Not everyone deserves all of your time, energy and love. When you realise you are a rare sort of person, with a lot to give, you will be more careful about who you surround yourself with.

There are more like-minded loving souls out there. Hold on for them. Don't waste your energy on people that have no intentions of appreciating and reciprocating it. You deserve to be appreciated. You deserve reciprocity. You deserve to be cherished.

Maybe 'rest' isn't working for you because what you actually need is movement. Not rushed movement but mindful movement. Maybe you need a gentle walk in the park with your phone on do not disturb. Maybe you need to swim in a stream or stretch your body in the sun. Laying in bed isn't always restorative when you feel stuck in your head and paralysed by the anxiety of all that you have to do when you get up. Let your mind, body and spirit rest in the very human nature of movement. Grounded in the presence of being alive.

Right now, that rejection letter or being laid off hurts like hell. You can't see yourself being as intimate with anyone else other than the person that left you. It feels so lonely not being accepted into that group of friends. You feel like you're not good enough, and that you never will be.

After a significant amount of time passes, you'll look back and realise that it wasn't about your worth. It was that those things, places, people and situations weren't meant for you. Something more aligned was meant for you. People that love you 10 times more and make you laugh 10 times harder. A job that truly values you and all the effort you put in. A place where you feel welcome, where you feel at home. Good people deserve good things. And to receive those good things you have to be willing to let go of everything that no longer serves you, everything that makes you question your worth. Those things you're holding onto are blocking the space needed for new things to enter your life. Rejection is redirection.

You cannot hate yourself into a version of yourself that you love. You'll be on a never-ending journey of self-improvement, you'll never feel good enough.

You may think, well I don't like this version of me, this version of me doesn't do the things I want to do, this version is horrible and lazy and keeps messing up.

No, this version is trying its very best to keep you alive throughout all the exhaustion and pain they've been through. They deserve credit for that.

Start with acceptance of where you're at. Appreciation of all that you've been through. Forgiveness for all that you didn't do and all the mistakes that you learned from. Every version of you deserves love because they are just trying their very best to survive.

Oh my goodness love you have the weight of the world on your shoulders and a million different things on your mind and you're racing around like you need to achieve something larger than life.

Slow down. Be kind to yourself. You do not have to have this all figured out in one night. You have time. You can change your mind. These feelings will not last forever. Give yourself grace.

That's a lot to carry all by yourself, it's okay to set it all down for a little while.

Maybe you've never been told this before but you're allowed to treat yourself like a best friend or a lover. You don't have to be at war with yourself 24/7.

You can make yourself cups of tea and write yourself uplifting notes. You can buy yourself a cupcake just because you're having a bad day or you're proud of something you ticked off of your to-do list. You can buy yourself those flowers just because they brighten up your day. You can write yourself a birthday card to open next year. You can run yourself a hot bath. You don't have to save those clothes that make you feel good for a special occasion. You can compliment yourself too.

You're allowed to do things that bring you joy. It's not selfish and it's not cringy. It's an act of kindness in a world that can be so harsh. You're allowed to look out for you too.

After a long period of numbness, emptiness or dissociation, you may have to re-teach yourself what different emotions and sensations in your body are.

Those feelings may be unfamiliar to you now. You may have to slow down and be very present to understand them. To watch a sunset with a loved one and think 'oh this is peace, this is joy.' Or even when you catch yourself crying you have to realise 'this is sadness, I am tired and sad.'

This was one of the most confusing and overwhelming parts of my healing journey. It's like the healing that comes after the healing. When you've felt nothing for so long, it can be hard to feel everything all at once. It's actually quite frightening. But you can do it. You can learn how to feel things again. It's safe to do so.

It's okay if you need to cry on your birthday every year. It's okay if you feel empty and alone during the holiday seasons. It's okay if you cannot feel the excitement others feel when autumn or summer comes back around.

Grief, heartbreak, fear of failure, fear of running out of time, financial issues, work stress, school stress, coming from a broken home, mental illness, physical illness, trauma, big life changes. All of these things can co-exist with candles on a cake and pretty lights on a tree. They don't magically go away because everyone else is suddenly having a fun time.

You're not broken for feeling the way you do. I hope one day you can feel the joy again. But for right now, it's okay to just let yourself be. You've been through a lot and forcing yourself to put on a fake smile to keep others happy is a lot of pressure to put on yourself.

It's really not surprising how much time we spend looking at screens and shaming yourself for it is not helpful. We have this small device that allows us to find out about almost anything in this life. Within seconds we can go to any place, play any game, connect with any person around the world, all from the comfort of our own homes. It is mental teleportation.

In a world that can be so harsh and chaotic, can we blame ourselves for wanting to escape and for creating our own online worlds so we can find a sense of control?

However, let's not forget to set them down from time to time to appreciate all that is good in the world. The sunrises and the sunsets. The changing seasons. The funny creatures roaming this earth alongside us. The new life that springs up out of seemingly nowhere. The communities and acts of kindness. The love that humans share. The moon and the stars. The hundreds of thousands of books written by people from all walks of life. All of the artwork and artefacts stored in museums.

The comfort of our own homes. The sound of children laughing and running around free without a care in the world. All of the water and different foods and flavours from around the world we have access to.

There is beauty to be found everywhere when we take a step back and become truly present in our surroundings.

If you're looking for a sign to let go, this is it.

You've been too patient with them for too long.

You've sent one too many texts.

You've communicated more than you needed to.

You've put your life on hold for them.

You've made one too many excuses for them.

Take back your energy love. It's not worth it.

I know how hard it is when you see so much potential in someone, as a romantic partner or a friend. If you've communicated your needs several times and they say they will change but then their actions never align with their words. It's time you really honour yourself and listen to that. You're holding onto who they could be, not who they are. No amount of asking will change them. Maybe they're not a bad person, they might just not have the emotional capacity to show up for other people right now. And if that's the case, you're going to destroy your mental health if you keep waiting on them, hoping you'll see the changes one day. You could be feeling this exact same way in months, years or even decades if you don't walk away. There is no guarantee they will change. Communicating more to make up for their lack of communication isn't going to work. Loving them more to make up for their lack of love isn't going to work. Giving them more attention to make up for their lack of attention isn't going to work. It's time to take back your energy and your power and walk away.

Trust the process. Trust all of the hard work you've put in. Trust all of the healing you've done. Trust yourself. Trust the universe. Even if you're not spiritual. Why? Because you need to trust that everything you've been working towards is going to create a beautiful life for you. If you don't trust this, then you're going to give up on yourself. You're going to go running back to the things that drain you and the people that hurt you. You're going to think, well it's too much effort so I might as well go back to my old ways of being.

You owe it to yourself to keep trusting and trusting until you see all of your hard work paid off. So you can prove to yourself that this wasn't all for nothing. There's no way you went through all of that emotional turmoil just to go back to the same problems, the same patterns. You're a better person now and you're creating a better life for yourself. Don't you dare go back. You've come too far now. You deserve all of the blessings that are coming your way.

I'm really proud of you. I think it's incredibly brave of you to get up every morning, despite everything you've been through. To show up in the world with nothing but good intentions for yourself and others. That's really a beautiful and rare quality to have. Not just resilience, but empathy, hope, a willingness to create a better life. You're the kind of person that chooses to heal instead of hurt others, which makes you one of those special people that makes this world a lovelier place to live in. People feel safe around you. You inspire people with all the light you bring.

Maybe you feel lost because you're desperately trying to find and reunite with a past version of you that your body and soul has vastly outgrown. Maybe you feel lost because you can see the potential of a future you, a version of you that is healed and happy but they feel so out of reach. You feel so stuck in this tug of war between your past self and future self and you forget to recognise the you that is now. Present self. The you that has shed old layers and is getting ready to step into the new. The version of you that exists right now is just as significant as any other version. You've learned how to let go of what was, and that is powerful. And you're learning just how vast your potential is, and that can feel overwhelming. These are two great life lessons that you have learned, and now is the time to find comfort in the space that lies in between. Let yourself ease into this potential. Step by step. Day by day. And one day, not too far into the future, you'll wake up, and you'll feel whole once again.

How are you doing?

No.

How are you *really* doing?

You may be able to lie to the world, politely tell them that you are fine. But we don't do pleasantries and fake smiles over here. Tell me how you really feel. And don't miss out all of the bits that feel messy and embarrassing and shameful. You're not too much and it's not too complicated.

Grab a piece of paper and write it all down. Vent to me. I don't care how cringy it feels. You're killing yourself trying to carry all of that weight by yourself. Set it down. Cry it out. Write down all of the anger, all of the frustration, all of the injustice. Tell me about all of it. I want you to tell me every last thing that's been holding you hostage recently.

Sweetheart, you may not want to hear this, but every time you say yes to doing something you don't want to do for other people, you're saying no to yourself. You're disrespecting yourself and your own needs.

Of course, you should do nice things for other people. But not because you think you have to. Not out of a false sense of duty. You do not have to say yes to everyone just to be polite. You're going to build up so much resentment and hit burnout. Then you physically can't do anything for anyone anymore, not even yourself.

You're a human being too and you're just as valuable as any other being. Stop being disposable to people that don't appreciate all that you do for them. It's not healthy. Sacrificing yourself for the title of 'polite' is not worth it. Any respectable person won't hold your no against you, and if they do, so be it. Let them think you're rude. I know, and you know, that you have a heart of gold and that's all that matters.

I will be honest with you, when you heal, you will most likely lose people. There is no way to sugarcoat it. It hurts your heart. It leaves you feeling so alone and defeated. But with every loss comes a huge gain. Realising your value is irreplaceable. Outgrowing people and letting them go is healthy. Quality is so much more important than quantity. It only takes one person that can truly see you, and love you as you are to truly comprehend how important quality connections are. Most significantly though, you won't lose yourself in other people anymore. You will forever have yourself.

At the end of the day, you have zero control over how other people perceive you. They only see what you present. And then, that's still limited by their own assumptions and perspectives on life. So you might as well show your true colours and be the person you want to be anyway. You can be rejected for trying to be someone you're not just as much as you can be rejected for who you truly are. You're allowed to grow and make changes. You don't have to keep justifying that to anyone. It's easier for people that you truly align with to come into your life when you're being true to yourself.

I know your mind feels foggy, your whole body aches and you don't have an ounce of enthusiasm left inside of you. You feel disconnected and you don't know how you're going to make it through another day.

You can, and you will.

I know this because I've been you. I was you for years and years. But there was a tiny voice inside of me that told me to keep going, and that it will get better one day. And that voice got louder and louder, the more I believed that I could start creating a beautiful life for myself. I can start whilst I'm tired. I can start from nothing. I can build myself back up, one day at a time.

You can do it and you will do it.

Listen to that inner wisdom.

Just focus on one day at a time. And if you can't do that, just focus on one hour at a time. And if you can't do that just focus on one minute at a time. And if that still feels too much, just focus on one second at a time.

You do not have to do everything all at once. The only moment that exists is this very second right now. All of the seconds in the future do not exist in your reality yet. So you don't need to worry about those. Just focus on what you need to do moment by moment to get yourself to where you need to be.

If you're grieving right now, my heart really goes out to you. I need to remind you that you are so incredibly loved regardless of how you feel. Healing takes time and you deserve all of the patience in the world. If I were with you right now, I would sit in comfortable silence, or offer a shoulder to cry on. I'd make you your favourite drink and something nice to eat. I'd hold you for as long as you needed. I'd sit for hours as you tell me stories and show me photographs. Or if you needed to be alone I'd leave you alone. I wouldn't take it personally. Your needs aren't too much. You deserve all of this gentleness and love. I'm sorry I can't be there for you in person right now, but just know my heart is with you. This same gentleness and love is within you. Treat yourself how I would treat you. With unconditional acceptance, with gentleness, with grace, with patience, with love. I'm sending you all of the love you need.

Someone not being able to or willing to meet your needs is no reflection of your worth. You're not asking for too much. You're simply asking someone that cannot, for whatever reason, give you what you need right now. You will lose your voice if you keep begging to be heard by someone that is not willing to hear you right now. They drown out the noise, and they may not even be doing it intentionally. Let go. Move forward.

There are people out there willing to give you everything you've ever asked for. And you may not even have to ask them for it. They are just healed and aligned and ready to pour so much love into another human.

Waiting for closure is prolonging heartache. What are you waiting for them to say? That they are sorry? That you are lovable and it's not your fault?

The hard truth is you may never receive closure from them. And even if you do, it might not be what you wanted to hear.

No closure is closure. Don't take it personally. Close the door yourself and move forward knowing you deserved clearer communication than that. There is so much more to life than waiting around hoping for the person that hurt you to come back and heal you.

There are many self-help books, therapists and spiritual teachers that will do more damage to your mental health than good. Those people that say you just need to think positive thoughts and have good vibes are contributing to toxic positivity. You're not a bad person for having painful emotions and negative thoughts. You can absolutely work on changing your beliefs, but it's not healthy to ignore how you feel. Imagine a friend came to you saying they were hurt and needed to talk through it and you told them to 'just be happy.' That's what you're doing to yourself when you listen to this false narrative that you can simply choose every thought. Process your emotions knowing that you can feel better and think nicer thoughts, but you're also allowed to feel how you feel right now. Emotions and thoughts are merely indicators of what has harmed you and where you need to heal. Lying to yourself isn't going to work. You don't have to agree with a person just because they have a degree or large following, especially not someone telling you how you're supposed to feel. You feel how you feel. It's really as simple as that.

What did you lose? Someone that wasn't showing up for you? Someone that made you feel hard to love? Someone that didn't have the emotional capacity to sustain a healthy relationship with you?

And what did they lose? Someone with a big heart that was willing to do whatever it takes to make it work? Someone that despite everything still sees the best in everyone? Someone that can be effortlessly loyal?

It's not a competition, but I say this for you to take that hurtful person off of the pedestal, and realise your own worth and value. Your loss was actually a huge gain.

You're not more lovable when you lose weight.

You're not more lovable when you get better grades.

You're not more lovable when you earn more money.

You're not more lovable when you achieve something outside of you.

Anyone that loves you based on your external achievements is loving you conditionally. You deserve unconditional love. You deserve to be loved based on the core of who you are, instead of the things that can be changed or be taken away.

Other people's inability to love unconditionally is no reflection of your worth.

People can love you or leave you, but they should never try to change you into their own limited narrative of what is lovable to them.

This might be a hard pill to swallow but you are not responsible for your emotionally immature parents. They are adults and they are responsible for their own feelings and behaviours. Just as you are responsible for yours. If they brought you into this planet to only love you conditionally, when you match their narrative of who you should be, that is a them problem, not a you problem. You did deserve to be born into unconditional love and you're not a failure or a burden if you do not live up to their expectations. You are an individual with autonomy and the ability to think and make decisions separately, you are not an extension of them.

In the same way you do not have to agree with them, they do not have to agree with you. However, that doesn't give them the right to then emotionally abuse you. I'm sorry if this has been your experience.

One day, you will look back at that person and you will see how they weren't right for you. You will see how they mistreated you and how powerful your potential is without them in your life. But for now, take care of yourself, treat yourself like a best friend that's just been heartbroken. The more love and trust you pour into yourself and your own life, the sooner that day will come.

If you were the 'quiet and mature' kid in school, that the teacher used as a model student, I am sorry. You were just a kid and you shouldn't have been isolated from the others like that. You shouldn't have always been sat by the 'misbehaving' kids to make them behave. You were not a co-worker. You may now hold the assumption that you're only lovable when you are quiet and 'well-behaved.' I'm here to tell you that you're allowed to speak up for yourself, make mistakes and take up space.

If you were the 'loud and immature' kid in school, that the teacher used to shout at and use as an example of what not to be, I am sorry. You were just a kid and you shouldn't have been isolated from others like that. You should've been taught how to handle your big feelings and energetic outbursts. You may now hold the assumption that you are annoying and a burden. I'm here to tell you that you didn't deserve to be shouted at, you're not a bad person and you can use that energy to achieve extraordinary things.

Children should not be used as behaviour markers. Every child is an individual human worthy of love and acceptance as they are. It is our responsibility as adults to teach them how to navigate their big emotions, behaviours and energy levels. Not to compare them to one another, to shame or embarrass them. Their brains haven't even fully developed yet. Telling kids they would be better if they acted more like this one child, creates separation. Alienation. Shouting at children that do not fit into a system that wasn't designed with them in mind is not 'behaviour management,' it's setting them up to feel worthless and incapable as adults.

Just because shouting and abuse was the norm when you were in school, does not mean it was okay. It has created mentally unhealthy anxious and depressed adults that do not function well in social situations or the workplace.

You self-sabotage to stay safe. Just as you're about to achieve or receive something good, you put an obstacle in the way. You run away or ruin it. Why? Because of all of your limiting beliefs, that you don't deserve it, that someone like you can't have that. You fear if you experience something good, now you just have something you can lose, something that can cause you a great deal of pain later on.

Let me tell you, you are worthy of good things and you are more than capable of opening up your heart and mind to receive them. Self-rejection is going to damage you way more in the long-run than being rejected by others. When you deny yourself the opportunities, the love, the job, the success, whatever it is, you're rejecting yourself before anyone or anything else has the opportunity to. Next time you get the urge to run, or hide, or destroy, take a step back, just breathe. And tell yourself, 'I deserve this and I give myself permission to lean into this.' Keep practising until experiencing good things feels natural to you.

You don't have to psychoanalyse every feeling. Yes, it's great to have an awareness of the root cause of your pain. It allows you to recognise unhealthy and toxic patterns in your life. However, you are also allowed to just feel your feelings without attaching a story. You can allow yourself to feel sad and just sit with it for a while. No thoughts, just sadness. You don't have to intellectualise every emotion. It will pass.

Depression can look like bed sheets unwashed for months, hair that's going to take hours to de-tangle and piles of rubbish everywhere. It can be unfinished assignments and unanswered text messages. Missed deadlines and darkness. Isolation. Chores left undone for months.

Depression can also look like bed sheets washed every week, a fresh put-together hairstyle and an immaculately clean home. It can be assignments and deadlines always met. Texts and emails always answered. It can be a beaming smile and perfectly scheduled calendar. Life of the party.

We cannot always assume people's inner state from their outer world. Some people cope by doing nothing. Other people cope by doing everything. Neither is more or less valid or more or less worthy of attention than the other.

Depression is depression even when it doesn't fit the stereotypical narrative.

So what do you do on those days where you are so depressed that you cannot get out of bed, but you know you'll feel better once you clean up your space and tick off your to-dos.

You do it one tiny action at a time. You don't go and take a shower. You only need to pull the covers off. Then all you need to do is stand up. Then all you need to do is walk to the bathroom. Then all you need to do is undress. Then all you need to do is turn the water on. Then all you need to do is set the temperature. Then all you need to do is stand under the water. Then all you need to do is squeeze the shampoo into your hands. Then all you need to do is rub it on your head. Do you get the point? I don't say this to patronise you, I say this because I understand how monumentous these everyday tasks feel. Break it down into the most do-able steps possible then congratulate yourself for each movement taken, you are building momentum and that's something to be proud of. That's your way forward. One tiny step at a time.

That indescribable sadness you feel in the pit of your stomach might be your inner child waiting to be held. To be heard. To feel seen.

If you find no other cause, look inward. Write a letter to your younger self and allow them to respond. Find them in your mind, where are they? Who are they with? What is hurting them?

Let them know you hear them. You see them. You love them. Explain to them that what they have been through is not their fault and you're dealing with it now. Take that burden away from them.

Take their hand and lead them away from that painful scene on repeat. Place them in a protective bubble with all of their favourite things. A beach or a park or a meadow. Now you can go on about your day knowing they are not in the places that hurt them, they are in a place that will heal them. A place where they can be free.

Those people that say it how it is, with the best intentions for you, are invaluable. The friends that aren't afraid to call you out on your unhealthy behaviours or point out when someone you love is treating you badly. No sugarcoating, no sass, just brutal honesty. It might sting for a while, you may want to defend yourself or the person hurting you, but you know in your heart that this friend is right. Thank this person, because there's not many like them, and they'll save you more than once. They'll hold you accountable. They'll keep you afloat. They'll point out what you refuse to see. And if you're one of those people, thank you, I appreciate you.

11:11

Here's my wish for you.

I wish for you to heal from whatever has hurt you.
I wish for you to experience healthy, unconditional love.
I wish for you to have financial stability and safety.
I wish for you to have friends that understand you.
I wish for you to find things that light you up inside.

Most importantly, I wish for you to find inner-peace, to end the internal battle you have with your painful past and your fear of the future. I wish for you to find all of the joy there is to be had in the present.

If you are someone that tells the world that you don't feel much, nothing really bothers you, but then you get overwhelmingly angry at the smallest things; a spilled drink, a mediocre driver, a small mistake at work, let me tell you, you have likely been severely wronged by the world, and you do feel deeply.

Every suppressed emotion takes its opportunity to come running out whenever there is a minor inconvenience. Any excuse to come to the surface, to be recognised.

I imagine you have either grown up being told that emotions are a weakness and to get on with life and you feel a great deal of shame, or your pain is so deep that you are afraid to look at it head on. Perhaps both.

Perhaps you feel a lot of fear, shame and pain. Maybe you drown it all in work, or alcohol or drugs. That only works for so long. Let me remind you, you are capable and strong enough to uncover everything you have kept hidden for so long.

How much of your pain is self-inflicted and how much is caused by others?

I am sorry to call you out, but you will never feel better if you think you can heal from what others have said or done to you whilst you're still currently at war with yourself. You need to look out for you. You need to help you. You need to be the one to practise speaking to yourself in a kinder way and managing the behaviours that are keeping you stuck.

Did you ever consider that you're not unworthy, broken, a burden, useless and incapable? But actually, the system you've been put in is worthless, broken, a burden, useless and incapable?

You've been forced to survive in a system that only allows a small percentage of the population to thrive, and even then, they still have their struggles.

Your needs, as a human being, are so much more important than the needs of any system that was not designed to serve you. Not everything you do needs to be about being a 'productive member of society.' As long as you're not hurting anyone, you can do things just because they bring you joy, even if they don't make sense to other people. This life is for you to live, not to serve a society that does not serve you.

Gentle reminders:

Your feelings are valid.

You deserve to feel loved.

You deserve to find inner-peace.

You are allowed to change your mind.

Your heart won't feel so heavy one day.

You don't have to explain yourself to everyone.

You don't need to be liked by everyone.

You are capable of doing that thing.

You can do what's best for you.

You can slow down.

My heart goes out to anyone that's spent their life knowing nothing but pure financial stress. Just trying to survive. No matter what anyone says to you, that's not fair. No one should have to sacrifice their mental and physical well-being just to put a roof over their head and food on the table. Everyone deserves to have their basic needs met and you're not a failure for struggling to do that. You shouldn't have to live in survival mode. You deserve financial stability, safety and quality time with your loved ones. I'm sorry the world has made you feel otherwise. People are not paid fairly for all of the hard work and hours they put in and that's not your fault.

I know how desperately you want somebody to validate you, to tell you what you need to hear. But when you go around asking everyone else's opinions on your idea, or your life, your head will become clouded. Everyone has a different perspective and it will only add to the internal conflict. You know what's best for you and you have to trust that vision. Even if things end up going wrong, you get to learn from your own mistakes. Following a particular piece of advice may be positively life-changing for one person, yet may be another person's greatest downfall. Trust your inner wisdom to guide you to where you need to go. Even if it turns out to be another learning curve. You'll get to where you need to be.

If you've ever been put in a situation where the consequences of saying 'no' to somebody frightened you more than the pain you had to endure by going along with what they wanted from you, I am so sorry.

You deserve to feel safe in your decisions and if someone forced you, blackmailed you, threatened you or just made you feel uncomfortable, to get consent out of you, that was not consent and that was not your fault.

I see you, I believe you and I'm sending you all of my love. It's time to forgive yourself now. That was not your fault.

You're allowed to take up space. As you are. As you've always been. You can let go of this belief that you must make yourself small, as to not inconvenience others.

They are the real inconvenience for making you feel as if you must live your life that way.

Take up space, love.

Spend a day walking around, seeing adults composed of little children trapped inside a tired adult's body. Including your own.

You will soon see the world in a different way. You will feel melancholy but you will also have more patience for others. More patience for yourself. Almost everyone has pain that has gone unnoticed for many years. Pain which they project onto others. Pain which they don't know how to let go of.

There is, however, hope. Because there's also a great deal of people choosing to heal. Don't lose sight of those people, they are a light in this world and so are you.

Loneliness itself is a lonely feeling. You feel like no one understands what you are going through but many people do. Many people have felt the emptiness and sadness of loneliness, it's just not often spoken about. Loneliness is isolating because not enough people talk about it. It's a vicious cycle. If you feel lonely, just know, you are not alone in that experience. It's more common than you realise, regardless of your age. Loneliness is not a feeling reserved for the elderly and widowed. Loneliness does not discriminate. You can be surrounded by people and still feel lonely.

Don't let the 'love yourself' message take away from the desire to experience love in other ways. You deserve to find and prioritise love within yourself first. But don't let this create feelings of shame when you crave family love, community love, romantic love and platonic love.

There are a million and one ways to experience love and you're not limited to only self-love. Self-love does not need to be as isolating as everyone makes it out to be. Self-love and all other forms of love can co-exist. When you learn to love yourself first, you'll find it easier to let others love you without limitations.

Internal love invites more external love into your life.

Sometimes heartbreak, trauma and grief can linger for longer than you were expecting because you feel the pressure to heal quickly and quietly. There is no timeline for healing. You can take as long as you need.

As long as you are allowing yourself to feel your feelings and keep moving forward, you are doing enough. The more you resist it and tell yourself you should be better by now, the longer it will take to heal.

Give yourself time.

If you are someone that has taken the time out to truly focus on healing and become a better person, instead of diving head-first into another relationship, you are incredible. I am so proud of you and I know how hard that is to do. It takes a lot of self-awareness and honesty. Especially when you crave closeness, connection and intimacy with another.

So many people avoid their problems and bring their pain into another relationship and the unhealthy patterns continue. You're breaking that cycle.

A big congratulations to you.

Self-care doesn't have to be bubble baths and roses.

Self-care can be doing the difficult things that future you will thank you for. Self-care is simply taking care of self and that sometimes means doing the more difficult things you don't feel like doing. Setting boundaries. Taking care of your finances. Booking that appointment.

Self-care has been capitalised and that will make you feel like you need to buy tons of products to feel better about yourself. Sometimes the root cause of the internal conflict is coming from all of the things you've been avoiding doing.

Do what's best for future you.

You deserve to feel safe. You deserve to feel safe in your home. In your body. In your mind. In your relationships. In your workplace. Wherever you are, whoever you are with, you deserve to feel safe.

I'm sorry if safety is a foreign feeling for you because you really do deserve it.

If you find it difficult to form new connections, I see you. It is terrifying to open yourself up and become vulnerable again. Especially after you've been hurt many times, you don't know who you can trust. Who will accept you for who you are vs. who will judge you and leave. However, you do deserve those close connections, and sometimes they're on the other side of fear. Trust yourself to choose the right relationships, even if that means going through a lot of the wrong people to find the right ones. There are billions of people on this planet. There are people out there that will understand you and love you just as you are.

Not all of the people or places you feel the need to let go of are 'unhealthy' or 'toxic.' It can be as simple as knowing your paths no longer align, a need to go on a separate journey even if the destination is ultimately the same. That need won't go away but you can always reunite with the same people and places later on if it's meant to be. You can go back home and you can message that person to reconnect one day. You can follow your own path and love people and places from a distance. We need to be more careful not to label everything as 'toxic' just because we've outgrown them. Sometimes it's not about them, sometimes the only unhealthy thing is the simple fact that we keep holding ourselves back from letting go and moving forwards.

You deserve someone who is kind. Someone who is gentle with your mind and body. Someone who takes the time to get to know you. Someone who loves you for your soul. Someone who communicates consistently and reminds you everyday of just how loved you are. Someone who is proud of you, even on your worst days. Someone who always shows up for you. Someone who really listens and makes you feel seen. Someone who remembers the little details about you. Someone who makes you a priority. Someone who respects you and loves you for who you are.

And more than anything, you deserve to become that 'someone' for yourself.

People reach a certain level of awareness, usually after a heartbreak or significant life event that shakes their current reality so strongly that there is no going back. And oftentimes they feel alone and misunderstood because they're no longer surrounded by people that have shared experiences with them. They're used to being with people that can relate to them. But how can they relate now that their whole world has been turned upside down? That's why it's so important to open up and become vulnerable instead of shutting down and closing yourself off. When you open yourself up, when you talk about your experiences, you'll find people that truly understand. That can guide you through the pain. I think that's why the best therapists, the strongest leaders and the most emotionally healthy people have often been through hell. It takes a certain type of person to go through so much pain and come out of it desiring to help others. And if you ask them what the hardest part was, it's often not the life-changing event itself, but the healing that came after. The feeling of aloneness and hopelessness in their struggle.

Give yourself credit. For all of the hard work you've put in. For all of the dark thoughts and emotions you navigate yourself through. For all of the times you stayed patient when every cell in your body wanted to scream. It doesn't matter if you feel like you haven't done enough yet. Giving yourself credit will make you feel empowered to keep moving forwards.

The stomach aches. The tight chest. The shortness of breath. The digestive issues. Full body exhaustion. Random aches and pains. The dull skin and fragile body. The headaches and irritability.

Not enough people speak about the physical effects of mental health issues and stress. They are very real and they make you feel as if you are unwell all of the time. You're not crazy, delusional or dramatic if the doctors cannot find any cause for your physical symptoms.

There's a high chance your body is under a lot of stress. Treat yourself with the same compassion and care you would a friend that's under the weather. Stop expecting yourself to perform to the same level that mentally healthy people do.

If you've ever felt that debilitating, persistent anxiety in your chest or stomach, I understand your discomfort. The constant hypervigilance and high alert when all you want to do is rest is exhausting. You may be in flight, fight or freeze mode. Survival mode. Remind your body that you are safe right now and can handle anything that comes up. Don't stress yourself about future problems.

I know it's easier said than done. But all you need to do at any given moment is focus wholeheartedly on the present moment, the current task at hand. Keep repeating that for each moment that passes. Trust your future self to handle any future problems at the time of happening. That way you're not tiring yourself by solving hypothetical scenarios that may never happen. Anything else that loops in your mind, write it down for later, free up that mental and emotional energy.

Sometimes you don't need to delve deep into the darkness to heal. Some days you just need lightness. A funny movie. Sweet texts to your friends. Your favourite snacks. A warm mug of tea. Quiet moments in nature. Some days you do need to switch off and experience the gentleness of the world and that's perfectly okay. Healing is about finding the light and sometimes all you need is those little wholesome moments that pull you out of the dark.

'Just don't worry about it' is so unhelpful because then you begin to worry about the fact you're worrying about it. You're allowed to worry about it. You're human. Work on becoming more grounded instead of eradicating all worries. The latter is a near-impossible task, fear is a survival mechanism and will always exist. Instead, allow yourself to feel where the anxiety is manifesting in your body. Notice your breath and what thoughts are coming up. Pretending your anxieties don't exist creates more anxiety. Having an awareness and acceptance of what's going on for you when those feelings arise will allow you to come back to the present moment and avoid creating a feedback loop of worries.

I know you think if that person that hurt you came back into your life and apologised you'd feel better but it would only be a temporary relief. That constant anxiety of them hurting you or leaving again would always simmer inside of you. It takes a lot of work to rebuild a strong level of trust between two people once it has been broken. Betrayal is not something that dissipates with a mere apology. There needs to be a consistent change in actions and behaviours. You're not weak for wanting someone you love back in your life. But you must recognise the strength in walking away from someone that cannot and will not change. Words are not enough.

You're not stuck. I know you think and feel like you are stuck, but you are not. It's an illusion. With persistence you can change your limiting-beliefs. And with changed beliefs comes a change of actions. You really can change your whole life around beginning with mere thought alone. You cannot completely eradicate negative thoughts and emotions but you can move towards a more open-minded and optimistic way of thinking.

That alone, after living your life expecting the worst, can set you free.

I know you want that apology. You want that person to sit down and acknowledge all of the pain they caused you and truly apologise.

The hard truth is, that may never happen. They may simply lack self-awareness, have no empathy or do not have the maturity to accept the consequences of facing their own demons and wrongdoings. They are safer hidden behind their web of lies.

The freeing truth is, you don't need them to admit to what they've done to feel validated. You know what happened to you and you know it wasn't your fault. That is enough. You're not crazy, delusional, sensitive or dramatic. If someone hurt you, they hurt you. End of.

You're allowed to take back power and validate your own suffering without the other admitting their wrongdoings. It doesn't matter what anyone else thinks, you know it hurts you. That quiet knowing is enough.

Not enough people speak of the taboo of grieving someone that is still alive. The loss of a person that can still be found. Whether it's a loved one that was abusive, crossing too many boundaries, or a person that for whatever reason isn't in your life in the same capacity anymore.

Distance and separation between family, friends or a partner can be freeing, isolating and suffocating all at once. Whether that person hurt you or not, you're entitled to grieve. Whether they played a role in the majority of your life or just a chapter, you're entitled to grieve.

Letting go of people is a life-changing occurrence and you don't have to pretend you don't feel a great loss. Even if the loss is merely the potential of who you thought they could be.

If you've ever been let down by the people that are supposed to be the most trustworthy in society, I hear you. Health professionals, teachers, carers, police workers and therapists can still hurt people. They can still break the rules that were put in place to protect you. They can neglect you, gaslight you and abuse you. I am so sorry if this is the case and it's hard for your voice to be heard because of their status. Their career shouldn't protect them from the accountability they owe you and everyone around you for their wrongdoings.

So if this is you, I believe you. I see you.

If you've ever attempted to voice your pain and been met with:

'You're being dramatic / over sensitive.'

'That never happened.'

'You just need to get over it.'

'Well I did my best, sorry I'm such a horrible person.'

'It's not that deep / you're overthinking it.'

'Why do you always have to bring this up?'

'I refuse to talk about it.'

'Never tell anyone that, you need to keep it quiet.'

'Just brush it under the rug.'

'You're weak, suck it up.'

'Men don't cry, man up.'

silence   *shouting*   *denial*   *anger*

I'm sorry. You deserved a more compassionate listening ear, validation and support moving forwards.

You're not broken.

Even when you feel empty, unseen and alone, you're still whole. Just like the moon, in all its phases.

When you see a moon crescent, you know the moon is not broken, it's partially concealed by the darkness.

The light can be taken from you but you're never broken. You may feel broken, but you are still one entity, hidden in the darkness for a little while.

This one is for all the tired parents. The single parents. The parents that are financially struggling. The parents that don't have a support system. The parents that are grieving. The parents that have little ones with health issues. The parents that need to be a carer to their adult children. The parents that are going through a divorce. The parents that have lost their homes. The parents that are struggling with mental and/or physical health issues. The parents that have to work non-stop to provide for their kids. Whatever your story, whatever your struggle, I have to remind you it's not a fancy home, car, holidays or expensive toys that make a good parent. It's unconditional love. It's the support and acceptance. It's the warm embrace you offer them. It's being their biggest supporter. It's the patience even when every ounce of you wants to scream. It's being able to listen to their feelings and apologise when you made a mistake. Give yourself grace as you navigate raising another human being. Don't forget to take care of yourself too.

There are many different causes of mental health issues and you don't have to listen to that one person that's convinced they know the one cause and solution to all of your problems. Mental health issues are incredibly multi-faceted and the causes can range from an enormous amount of childhood trauma to a slight vitamin deficiency or hormonal imbalance. There are many 'mental health professionals' that will tell you to simply switch off screens, exercise and eat healthier. You're not broken or doomed because those things didn't immediately eradicate all of your suffering. Those 'solutions' don't even take many disabled people or people with life-long genetic mental illnesses into consideration. It also invalidates people like athletes on strict exercise regimes and healthy diets that experience mental health issues. A textbook understanding of mental-health isn't always the solution to your pain. It is often the people that have experienced the darkness themselves that will be able to comprehend your struggles and help navigate you towards the genuine support and solutions you need.

There are people in this world I like to call 'the givers.'

They give their whole heart and more to the people that they love. They light up a room even when they're feeling low. They give endlessly even when the world doesn't give much back. Hold onto those people. Remember to thank them. Remember to give back.

If you're a giver, please give back to yourself. You deserve all of that love and kindness too. You are indeed a beautiful soul, but you must learn the art of pouring back into self. To celebrate your own achievements like you celebrate others. To give yourself gifts like you give to others. To be patient with yourself like you're patient with others. To be proud of yourself like you are proud of others. To believe in yourself like you believe in others. To forgive yourself like you forgive others. To love yourself like you love others.

Give back to you, my love, give back to you.

Stay for you.

If you've ever felt like ending your life, you know the drill. 'Oh but that's so selfish, stay for your family, stay for the people that love you, they will be so hurt and broken.'

It's infuriating because here you are, suffering so much, and the only reason you're given to stay is a guilt trip to avoid others from suffering too.

So stay for you. Stay because you deserve to heal. You deserve to experience how life feels on the other side of pain. Stay because you haven't seen the parts of the world you dream of seeing yet. Stay because you haven't seen all of the unreleased movies and songs that will become your new favourites one day. Stay because you are a beautiful soul, you're incredibly unique, and your existence is just as significant and worthy of living as anyone else's. Stay because you haven't met all of the people that love you yet. And stay because you haven't met all of the parts of yourself and your life that you love yet. Stay for you, my love. Stay for all of the things you are yet to experience. Stay because you know you can. Stay because you don't know what tomorrow can bring and it could change your life in the most incredible way. Stay because even if there's more pain, there will inevitably be more joy coming your way. And you deserve an abundance of it. Stay because you're curious. You deserve to see all of the extraordinary sights you haven't seen yet. You deserve to find comfort in the little things in life. You deserve to meet the version of you in the future, that is looking back on you now, cheering you on and thanking you for staying, because they got to experience all of those things that made it worth it. Stay for your inner-child that wants you to feel better, that wants you to feel safe and happy again. Stay for the new perspectives you'll gain on life. Stay for the potential. Stay because regardless of how you feel right now, suffering is temporary. You can build yourself up from the ground upwards. Stay for you.

There is gratitude and then there is toxic-positivity.

Gratitude is finding things that bring you comfort and joy, no matter how small. It's acknowledging and accepting that you are struggling but you can still find things you'd truly miss if you woke up tomorrow and they were gone.

Toxic-positivity is trying to turn every negative into a positive and completely bypassing your feelings and suffering. 'Just be happy.' 'Good vibes only.'

Ignore those people that tell you that you won't suffer if you were more grateful for what you had. You're entitled to feel your pain, it's part of the human experience and ignoring it will cause more problems and greater suffering in the long run.

Whenever you feel off track or triggered, keep asking yourself these questions:

'How would the version of me that loves and respects myself respond to this?'

'Does this support the life I'm trying to create?'

'What is my intuition / gut feeling trying to tell me about this situation?'

'Does this protect or destroy my inner-peace?'

'What would I tell my best-friend or younger self to do in this situation?'

'How much is this going to impact my quality of life in the future?'

Lovely, take a deep breath. Slow down.

Respond, slowly, intentionally.

Stop reacting quickly and irrationally. It hurts you.

I get it, you're upset, you're angry, you're triggered, you want to be heard, you want to get your point of view across.

You owe it to yourself to give your nervous system a chance to calm down. You owe it to yourself to respond in a way that helps instead of hinders the future version of you. You owe it to yourself to give yourself time to think this through calmly and rationally. You owe it to yourself so you can communicate clearly instead of saying something you may later deeply regret.

I don't care what anyone has told you, being a student is tough. Invalidating your struggles because someone found being a student easier than working or being a parent is not fair. The academic pressure, fear of failure, social anxiety, never-ending assignments, financial struggles and heaps of deadlines are enough to cause mental health issues. On top of this, you may not be eating or sleeping properly. You may have childhood trauma or problems at home. You may struggle to make friends. You may be going through a break-up. You may be disabled or have pre-existing mental-health issues. It's tough. And tiring. Don't listen to anyone telling you to get over it. They are not you and they are not experiencing the same struggles, thoughts and feelings that you are. As soon as you stop pretending it's all okay, the sooner you can reach out for the support you need. You deserve all the support you can get. And I'm proud of you regardless of how much of a failure or disappointment you may feel right now.

Sometimes a situationship can hurt more than a break-up. You're not just grieving the end of it, you're also grieving what could have been, the potential. You probably didn't get to the point in the relationship where you realise their flaws and what annoys you about them. You didn't get the commitment you really wanted. You didn't get the love you thought it could lead into.

And love, I know it sucks, but you have to let go. Loving them more and trying to change their mind isn't fair on either of you. Maybe they're unhealed or just not the right person for you. The reason for it not going further doesn't matter. You're worthy of that gentle, consistent, committed, safe love you've been craving. You're worthy of clarity instead of confusion.

Allow yourself to grieve it like it was an actual break-up, even if the people around you don't understand.
Cry it all out so you can move on with your life.

This may sound simple but you can ask people how they feel about you. You don't have to guess if they're angry or upset with you. You don't have to guess if they're interested in you or wasting your time. You're allowed to ask. You're allowed to tell people how their behaviours have been making you feel. You're allowed to gain clarity instead of making assumptions. And if they don't respond, that is an answer in itself.

Communication is healthy, but it goes both ways. You can ask to have a conversation. You don't have to wait for them to bring it up. You can tell them how you feel.

Unconditional love does not mean unconditional tolerance. You can have all of the love in the world for a person but if their behaviours or addictions are destroying your peace, you do not have to tolerate that.

It's time we normalise loving people from a safe distance. It doesn't make you a bad or hateful person to create distance. It doesn't make you a failure. You're not their therapist and it's not your responsibility to fix them. You are allowed to put boundaries and safety measures in place to protect yourself and your loved ones.

Humour and comedy is brilliant. Laughing is one of the greatest pleasures of life. But, and I'll be calling a lot of you out here, if you are laughing off your feelings instead of acknowledging them, hear me out. I get it, the self-deprecating and mental health jokes help you cope, they make you laugh through dark times. Imagine though if someone you care about came to you and told you they were really struggling, and you laughed in their face. How invalidating and awful that would feel for them. How guilty you'd feel.

Yeah well, you are kind of doing that to yourself. You are invalidating your own suffering. It's escapism at its finest. Some of the greatest comedians in the world were suicidal and went unnoticed because they were always the one lighting up the room. I don't want to take your comedy away from you, I bet you are hilarious, but if you struggle with talking about your emotions, I just want you to know that it's okay. There's room for you to be funny and to be cared for. You deserve help too.

Men do cry.

Men are allowed to cry.

Men that cry are masculine.

Men that talk about their feelings are strong.

Men that open up about mental health are important.

Men that struggle to talk about their feelings are valid.

Crying is human, not feminine.

Crying is healthy, not weak.

Crying is life-saving, not emasculating.

I'm sorry if you've ever been told that you're weak, or that men don't cry. They do. There's just so much stigma that some men have lost the ability to be able to cry when they need to. And the ones that do, do it behind closed doors.

You're allowed to cry, it doesn't make you any less of a man. It'll save you from so many pent up emotions that could lead to anger, mood swings or outbursts. Let yourself cry. It's easy to avoid your pain and project it onto others. It's hard to feel your feelings. So don't listen to those people that tell you crying is feminine and weak. They go around hurting other people instead of taking responsibility for their emotions, and that's the real weakness.

Emotional intelligence in a world that tells you to suck it up, is a true testimonial of strength.

If you act on impulse, I see you.

Set yourself this rule:

Never make permanent decisions based on temporary emotions or intrusive thoughts.

Give yourself time to weigh out the pros and cons.

Wait until you feel more stable, more grounded.

It might just save your life.

Reaching out for help is a great step forwards, but we can't keep ignoring the fact that the authorities behind mental health services and resources are failing us. Waiting lists are too long. Many people get referred to hospitals that aren't specialised in mental health support, leaving staff feeling overwhelmed and helpless. Private therapy isn't affordable or accessible to everyone. Many teens are told they're too old for child therapy yet too young for adult therapy, leaving them neglected. 1 hour of talking therapy a week isn't enough for some people that are in a very dark period of their life. Not everyone can comprehend all the different types of therapy and mental health resources and that different things work for different people. There's a lot of psychological jargon. Working ridiculous amounts of hours at school, work, as a carer or parent, and never having any time for self-care is detrimental to our mental health.

If you've repeatedly tried to get help and not received it, it's not your fault. The systems designed to help people are hindering them. Don't stop advocating for yourself.

You can feel angry, upset, grateful, relaxed, loving, resentful, tired, energised, underwhelmed and overwhelmed all at the same time.

Life throws many different blessings and challenges our way simultaneously so it makes sense that you feel a whole range of different emotions. It's very human.

Healing on your own before entering a new relationship is necessary to avoid bringing old problems into new places and you should be proud of yourself for taking that step. But please don't fall into the trap of thinking you must be perfectly healed and trigger-free before you can open up your heart again. We're always going to experience some negative emotions and triggers regardless of how much we've healed, there's no getting rid of them completely. A healthy relationship is one in which you can both hold space for one another to communicate openly and work through any triggers and emotions that come up. Both people need to be willing and able to have the patience and understanding to grow together. You can heal together in those types of connections.

I often see the phrase 'no one judges you more than you judge yourself' but actually some people do. You can reach such a place of self-acceptance and self-love where you no longer spend all day judging yourself. You just do you, without attaching any stories to it. And yet, some people still do everything in their power to make it obvious they disapprove of this and they are judging you. Your appearance. Your life choices. Your personality. Your beliefs. Whatever they can, they will judge. Oftentimes it's your own family or friends.

What matters is that you don't let it get to you anymore. You filter it all out because you can see it's a projection of their own lack of self-acceptance. Whether you decide to set boundaries with those people, ignore them or simply walk away is completely up to you. But don't let it take away all of the inner peace you have cultivated.

To all of the people from broken homes, I know you used to walk home at night, peering into the lit up windows full of families sitting round the table laughing and having dinner together, wondering why you didn't get that. It wasn't you. It wasn't your fault. You were never unworthy for having not experienced that. You deserved that just as much as the next person. It's okay if you need to grieve the family love and sense of home you never got to experience, or that for whatever reason got taken away from you.

There's nothing wrong with you if you never had that big friendship group, or those life long friends. Or if you had them and outgrew them. The truth is we don't always click with the people we're put into the same spaces as. The same family, school or workplace isn't always enough of a similarity to keep a connection going. Friendships take time and effort from both sides of the connection to maintain and some aren't worth holding onto for the sake of politeness. If you don't connect, you don't connect. It can be as simple as that. There are people that think and feel like you do, people with the same values, interests and sense of humour, you just haven't crossed paths yet.

What do you do when you still feel the heaviness and longing for a person that seems to have moved on?

You realise, them moving on is no reflection of your worth. That, it may just all be an illusion, or avoidance of feelings, but either way, that's not what matters right now. Making assumptions about how they feel is taking energy away from you, and what you feel.

Let go of the need to know, and redirect all of that attention to detail back to yourself. You have a big heart and a huge capacity to love, and that's a beautiful thing to discover about yourself. All of that love for them was coming from you, which means you have the capacity to love yourself that much.

Feel your feelings and pour all of that love back into yourself. It doesn't matter how they feel anymore, or how they move forward. All that matters is how you feel, how you move forward.

Thinking about work isn't taking a break from work. If you're thinking about work, you're still working. Give yourself permission to switch off and only think of the things that concern you and your personal life. I know it's hard when your mind is consumed with the stress of work. Especially if you're self-employed and your finances depend on you. But rest is important and productive. Connecting with yourself is important and productive. Spending quality time with loved ones is important and productive. It's okay to switch off, I promise it won't derail your success. Rest and connection will restore you and clear your head so you can go back to that work with more focus and energy.

You may have seen those quotes that say it's never too late because this extremely well-known celebrity or entrepreneur didn't make it until they were 30, 40, 50 and so on.

I think it's a great reminder that we can achieve success at any age.

However, we shouldn't re-enforce this idea that we're not significant or successful unless we achieve something that makes us known around the world.

We're not all meant to be extremely famous or create something life-changing. It takes away from the seemingly 'ordinary' people that have impacted lives.

The people that show up for their job, their loved ones or their community and make the word a better place to live in. Those people are just as worthy of recognition.

Some people will cause emotional turmoil because it's what they're used to. It makes them feel alive. It gives them an excuse to let out all of their feelings. It's their comfort zone. Those people that cause drama and create problems where there could easily be peace. Repeating unhealthy patterns for a sense of familiarity. Quietness would mean they have to look inwards, which is scary, so they're as loud and disruptive as possible. Blaming everyone else for problems they created. It's why many people self-sabotage healthy relationships and good opportunities. If you're reading this book, I imagine you had the self-awareness to break free from these cycles, or you at least try to. If that sounds like you, give yourself credit because if you look at those people now, you can see how blind-sighted they are by their own self-inflicted suffering. That used to be you. Now you're here. That's something worth celebrating. A huge sign of growth. If you're still working on it, this is your sign to keep moving forward, keep choosing to do the inner-work. It's all worth it in the end.

Many of the people that tell you that you're too emotional and too sensitive, ironically, are the same people that lack any sense of emotional control. They're usually the ones that have terrifying road rage or get into fights quickly. The ones with the bad temper, that see red and make impulsive, destructive decisions. The ones that hurt others instead of healing. The ones that shout and slam doors. Or they're the people that are passive aggressive and do silent treatment, which yes, is a huge emotional response.

So no, you're not too emotional or too sensitive for crying and acknowledging your hurt. It's so much wiser to have emotional intelligence and feel your feelings than it is to bottle them up and let them uncontrollably explode onto others.

Please, please, please, don't let your fears tear away the opportunity to experience a life you love.

Please recognise the people in your life that are trying to display healthy love and a deeper connection, before they get tired of overcompensating and leave.

Please recognise that if you weren't worthy of that degree, or that job, or that opportunity, that you wouldn't even have it in the first place.

You can be the person that works towards opening up your heart to healthy relationships and you can be the person that goes for that opportunity.

If you can't do it for present you, do it for future you. Do it because future you deserves the love and the life you've always dreamed of. Please don't self-sabotage good things just because you feel unworthy right now. You've punished yourself enough for one lifetime.

You're not perfect. They're not perfect either. No one is perfect. Perfect is an illusion. Everyone has different requirements for perfection, therefore it is unachievable for one person to be perfect to everyone else. You may be one person's idea of perfection, and another person's idea of chaos. Chasing perfection is a waste of energy. It's our differences that make us interesting and lovable. If we were all carbon-copies of one another, how would we choose who to love? We would have no sense of individuality. No ability to differentiate between others.

Go for personal progress, it's so much more achievable than conventional perfection.

'Love yourself.'

- *the society that shames any act of self-love*

Your insecurities are profitable. Anything you perceive as a flaw or problem within yourself, I can guarantee there's some stinking rich business man that has a product to change it.

Loving your insecurities is an act of rebellion against people that only care about money and power. Loving yourself makes others feel safe to do the same. Your loved ones will feel safer to let go of their insecurities when you lead by example. Do it for you, first and foremost, but notice how just by being yourself you provide a safe space for others to do the same.

It's a different approach to self-love, but it might just be the one you need, if you're the sort of person that likes to break the rules.

What they don't tell you when you begin learning about yourself is the amount of unlearning you have to do. It's messy and painful and confusing. Dismantling all of the thoughts and beliefs you no longer resonate with and then having to replace them with ones that do align with you and your values. That takes work and persistence, so be patient with yourself as you go through that process.

Lovely, it's okay to admit you're angry. If you have been wronged, abused, hurt, belittled, it's okay. Be angry.

Anger doesn't make you a horrible or hateful person. If you keep it bottled up inside you're going to accidentally let it out on somebody, then you really will feel guilty. Anger is healthy, keeping it simmering inside of you isn't.

Write a letter and rip it up. Channel the anger into something creative. Safely break something. Scream into a pillow. Cry it out. Scream off the top of a mountain. Dance it off. Go for a run or hike. Do a difficult workout. Stand up for causes you believe in. Vent to somebody you trust. Listen to songs that express how you feel.

As long as you're not harming others, do whatever you need to do, but please don't keep it inside.

It'll eat you alive.

Sweetheart if you wouldn't stand 3 inches away from your friend's face and pick out each and every single one of all of their 'flaws' for 10 minutes straight, please move away from the mirror.

The reflection you see is a human being, just like your friend, worthy of love and acceptance.

I promise you the vast majority of people do not care about or even notice those things you pick out in the mirror each day, and if they do, they're really not someone worth keeping around in your life.

You're so much more beautiful and complex than the superficiality of first appearances. Anyone that can't see further than skin deep needs a reality check.

You may never have been asked this before but what do you want?

Not what your parents want. Not what your friends want. Not what your teacher or boss expects of you. Not what your partner wants. Not what you think you should want based on your upbringing.

What do you want?

What came up first? Was it something material and physical like a home? Was it something intangible like inner-peace or feeling loved? Was it a dream or goal you've yet to achieve?

Your answer to that is what's heavy on your heart and as long as it's not intentionally hurting anyone, including yourself, I think you should go for it.

I don't think it's irrational to be emotionally unstable when life throws 50 things your way at the speed of light.

I also don't think it's irrational to be completely numb when life has exhausted you to the very max.

You absolutely deserve emotional stability but please don't shame yourself for what you cannot control.

Shaming yourself for having very human responses to a stressful life is only going to create more emotional instability and numbness. Let go of the judgement.

You're doing just fine.

If you have a lot to say to someone that's no longer in your life, whether it be love or hatred, write them a letter.

WAIT. I'm not done.

Do NOT send the letter. I repeat. Do NOT send the letter.

Write it out, don't hold back. But then rip it up, bury it or safely burn it.

Why aren't we sending it? Because this exercise is for you, not them. This is about your feelings and making yourself feel validated and seen. Their response may not be what you hoped for or needed. So do this one, just for you. Because you deserve to let out all of those unspoken words and give yourself the closure you need.

This is a hard truth to learn but you get to choose what you believe about yourself. Every day, you get to make the decision, am I going to be my own best friend or my biggest enemy today?

And of course, you may have unwanted feelings or intrusive thoughts that you do not control. But you are not those feelings or thoughts, you are the one that chooses to either dismiss or agree with those thoughts.

Choose the beliefs that uplift you and keep choosing them until it feels normal. Whether it takes you weeks or years for them to feel natural, it'll be worth it. It's so much easier to live your life rooting for yourself instead of plotting against yourself.

If you're an adult feeling like you're constantly in 'trouble' or about to be told off, I hear you. It can feel embarrassing to acknowledge or talk about because it's the type of fear a child has. The reality is, it probably is your inner-child feeling that way. It can make you feel incredibly on edge and paranoid. You may feel like you have to walk on eggshells or always be on your best behaviour. You're an adult now though and you have autonomy. Even if someone were to tell you off or shout at you, you wouldn't have to put up with that. You can stand up for that little child inside of you and set boundaries. No adult should be telling you off or shouting at you. They should be communicating calmly if they have an issue. It's a baseline level of respect. So take yourself out of the spotlight, make mistakes and take up space. It's okay. You're not in trouble.

Regardless of what anyone has told you:

You are allowed to make mistakes.

You are allowed to change your mind, your career path and your lifestyle.

You are allowed to choose your own beliefs.

Your sexuality is valid.

Your dreams are valid.

Your mental health is valid.

Your feelings are valid.

Your parents are not you, they do not have your mind, you are an individual that's allowed to make your own choices, even if they disagree with them.

Social media isn't just a highlight reel it's also a mask.

Behind that happy family photo there could be a lot of trauma and conflict.

Behind that cute couple photo there could be a lot of arguing and emotional abuse.

Behind that photo of a group of friends having the time of their lives there may be a lot of backstabbing, gossip and drama.

Behind that travel vlog there could be a lot of isolation, loneliness and running from problems.

Behind that clothing haul or new tech, there could be financial issues or shopping addiction.

Behind that selfie there could be a lot of body dysmorphia and insecurities.

We cannot comprehend the reality of anyone's life or true feelings from a bunch of photographs or videos on the internet, and nor should we. It's not healthy.

Social media is a great tool that keeps us connected from all around the world, but don't allow your own assumptions to create disharmony and disconnection from others. Their life may look perfect to you but they may be having the exact same feelings and problems that you are. They may look at someone else's highlight reel and compare it to their own, wishing they were in their shoes instead.

The never-ending comparison will destroy your peace and mental health and it's keeping all of us stuck, jealous, judgemental, bitter and disconnected.

Your body is just a shell. A moving home for your being. You deserve to experience the depth of life's experiences without worrying about the temporariness of how it looks. Your heart beats for you. It beats just for you, every moment of the day, 24/7, to experience life. Your heart doesn't work all day everyday for you to just stand in front of a mirror hating what you see. It beats so you can laugh, so you can cry, so you can see the world. So you can connect with others and create beautiful memories. Honour your heart and live life to its fullest without the added stress of how your body looks. Next time you want to go to the mirror to hate on yourself, place your hand on your heart instead. Feel your heartbeat and remember you're alive and you're loved and that's all that matters.

I asked a successful entrepreneur that had created multiple six-figure businesses this:

'What do you regret most about your journey getting to this point?'

Do you know what they told me? They wished they had slowed down. They regret not taking the time to enjoy the journey and process everyday. They said, they have the money and success now but life's not any different and they'll never get the lost time back. They'll never be able to go back and spend more quality time with their loved ones, to be more present and enjoy everything they were doing and learning.

This is quite the contrary to the usual narrative. It's a reminder not to rush through life trying to reach one destination thinking it'll bring you happiness, because you'll never get that time back. Appreciate all that you can in the present moment. Appreciate the growth and progress everyday.

Memory loss can be a protective mechanism.

If you know you had a difficult childhood, or were in an abusive relationship, but don't remember all of it, your trauma is still valid. Your own brain is protecting you from things probably best unknown. You don't have to remember everything for your feelings to be justified.

You can be traumatised and not fully comprehend why.

I don't blame you for expecting the worst when all you've ever been met with is disappointment after disappointment. But believing so is believing you have no control over your life. There will be things out of your control but there will also be many mindset shifts and behaviours you can implement to create a better quality of life. You don't have to be defined by your past experiences. You're allowed to start fresh, right now, and decide you're going to create a better life for yourself, no matter what it takes.

Rest can be lying in bed staring at the ceiling. Rest can be time in nature. Rest can be crying your eyes out. Rest can be laughing with loved ones. Rest can be taking a nap. Rest can be switching your phone onto do not disturb. Rest can be setting work boundaries so colleagues don't contact you outside of work hours. Rest can be letting the sun hit your skin. Rest can be watching the little raindrops run down your window. Rest can be a sick day. Rest can be watching a childhood favourite movie. Rest can be movement. Rest can be doing nothing but sitting in silence.

There are no rules for rest. Rest is whatever takes the weight off of your shoulders and restores your energy. Rest is productive. Rest is necessary for the human psyche. Burnout is no joke and can take years to truly recover from. Let yourself rest. Without rules and without limitations.

If you're going through a breakup, give yourself the breakup. Don't give them the same access to you as if you were in a relationship. Don't text them everyday. Don't sleep with them. Don't post things on social media to get their attention. Don't stalk them. Don't beg them. Don't manipulate them. You'll regret it. All of it.

Focusing all of your attention onto them is denying the separation. It hurts like hell but if you can accept the breakup now, it'll prevent you from having to face it later on. You're prolonging it. You can grieve now and in 3 months feel like a completely new person. Or you can hold onto something that isn't there anymore and in 3 months time you have to begin the grieving process. I know you probably hate me for saying this now but you'll thank me down the line when you look back and realise you didn't need them back, you just needed all of your own energy and attention to be poured back into you. Losing them is not as detrimental as losing yourself trying to convince them to come back.

Growth and new places can feel lonely, but so can staying in places you've outgrown. Nothing feels lonelier than stunting your own growth so as to not disturb others. If you want more for yourself, for your life, make room for it. Let go of all the people, things and situations holding you back. The people that are meant to be in your life will support your evolution.

You are not defined by your job or your family. You're so much more than your upbringing or career choice. Don't attach your identity to these things outside of you. You are you. Your past doesn't have to define you. Your circumstances don't have to define you. You can define you, you can define you based on whatever you feel to be true to you.

Your identity crisis can be fixed by simply acknowledging that you are you right now, and that is enough. You can learn about the rest along the way.

Cheating is never about you. Some of the most conventionally attractive, nicest, meanest, richest and poorest people in the world get cheated on. There is no common denominator other than the fact cheaters lack self-discipline, loyalty and responsibility for their actions. If they felt unsatisfied in themselves or the relationship for whatever reason, they had the choice to communicate with you and create solutions, or to leave you so you can heal in peace without being deceived.

I promise you, it's no reflection of you or your worth. If you agreed upon a monogamous relationship, you deserved the loyalty that was rightfully expected. If they could not give you the bare minimum level of respect, that's a huge indicator of their own personal problems and ego, and nothing to do with you. Adults are responsible for their behaviour. Stop making excuses for them. Stop blaming yourself. It's not your fault. You didn't need to be any more or any less of who you are.

Learn to apologise. Genuinely. Authentically. Sometimes we're the ones that need to learn to say sorry instead of brushing it under the rug. Sometimes we're the ones that hurt others, push their boundaries or react in an unfair way. Sometimes we make unfair assumptions about people or judge them. So put aside your ego, be honest with yourself and practise admitting and amending your wrongdoings. It'll heal your loved ones and set you free.

Your hobbies and interests aren't boring. Your dreams and goals aren't cringeworthy. You just haven't been surrounded by people that have the same appreciation for the same things you love and value. You don't have to abandon the things that light you up inside because other people don't understand them. Continue doing your thing and spend time in places you love and you'll eventually attract like-minded people.

Being a quiet introvert is difficult in a noisy world because it's socially acceptable for people to say 'you're too quiet,' 'speak up,' 'talk more,' 'cheer up,' and 'you're making it awkward.' It's not so socially acceptable to tell people 'you're too loud,' 'pipe down,' 'talk less,' 'stop being so cheerful' and 'you're making me uncomfortable.'

There's nothing wrong with sitting quietly without a great deal of expression if that's how you feel most comfortable. Don't mask and drain your energy to make other people happy when they don't hold space for you. It's okay to show up as you are. It's not rude to be yourself. It's rude for people to make you feel like you need to put on a performance for the sake of politeness.

Comparing a broken leg to a heart attack is pointless because they're completely separate issues with completely different treatments. So in the same way we don't compare physical health, let's stop comparing our mental health to others. Comparison isn't helpful. Acknowledgement and attention to detail is more important. It doesn't matter if you think someone else's ailment is worse, yours still needs healing before it worsens.

There is room for your creativity in this world. It's needed.

Artists. Poets. Writers. Leaders. Scientists. Inventors. Engineers. Photographers. Filmmakers. Surgeons. Designers. Architects. Coders. Teachers. Lawyers. Managers. Entrepreneurs. Psychologists. Analysts. The list of careers and places where your creativity is invaluable is endless.

Creativity is not limited to painting and drawing.

There's room for you too.

When you're ready to turn your day around:

Relax your jaw. Let your shoulders drop down. Take the deepest breath you've taken today. Spend a moment tidying your space. Stretch your arms up to the ceiling. Make your bed. Drink some water. Have a snack. Write down your feelings. Text somebody you love. Crack open a window. Put on a clean shirt. Listen to some uplifting or gentle music. Take a walk around the block.

It's the little things that can bring you back to the present moment and give you the biggest shift in momentum.

When was the last time you asked someone how they are doing? When was the last time someone asked you how you are doing? When was the last time you asked yourself how you are doing?

How are you doing?

How are you *really* doing?

If the world feels too heavy today and all you did was lie on your bed and stare up at the ceiling, that's okay.

Don't feel bad for it.

Acceptance will help you move past this exhaustion.

Feeling guilt and shame for simply existing and processing life will keep weighing you down and you'll never feel like getting up.

Let yourself be. It will pass. You'll get up again.

The world doesn't need you to be more like that person, it needs you to be more like you.

It's diversity and individuality that keeps us sane and interesting in a society that expects us to all be and act exactly the same.

It is diversity and individuality, wild ideas and outcasts that create the biggest change. New inventions. New masterpieces. New ways of thinking.

Other people can't see your vision because they're not you. You see your vision because it's meant for you. It doesn't make sense to anyone else because you were meant to act on it, not them.

Be you. Follow your vision.

Love, give yourself a break.

Switch off.

The world can wait.

Your well-being always comes first. You've always been enough. You don't have to prove that to anyone. It's innate. Rest shouldn't be met with hostility and judgement. Rest should be met with acceptance and kindness.

You are allowed to rest.

When you become overly emotionally attached to a person, a career, a job, a way of thinking, a location, or anything really, you're closing yourself off to the endless possibilities that could be available to you.

You're limiting your happiness and success to something so small and temporary when really, there are many different people you meet or paths you can take that bring you just as much, if not more, joy and fulfilment.

If a person or job doesn't work out. I promise you don't need them back to survive and be happy. It's a sign, pushing you in a new direction. To see that there is more out there for you. More that is aligned with you.

Don't feel like you're being unrealistic. You've been so trapped in one way of seeing the world for so long, you've neglected to see just how much can be achievable for you.

You might not need someone to tell you what to do. You might already know exactly what to do. You're just exhausted and terrified and need someone to stand by you as you do it. I'm sorry if there is no one there besides you. Support is important, you deserve that, but it might not be available to you right now.

If that's the case, I want you to know, from a distance, I'm rooting for you. I believe in you. You can do hard things. You can make mistakes and pick yourself back up again. You can try again as many times as you need to. Don't give up on yourself because there's no one there for you. Be the person you need right now.

Many people neglect to acknowledge that you can begin to feel emotionally stable again, for weeks, months, maybe even years, then hit a wall. You feel numb or low for no apparent reason.

Perhaps that reason is that you have finally been able to comprehend how life is meant to be for you. Peaceful, joyful, balanced, healthy relationships, boundaries, communication, self-love and compassion. And looking back makes you realise just how much of this your past self missed out on.

So then you might have to grieve that.

That's okay but don't go back.

Your past self did deserve this love and this life, but it was your past self that brought you here.

So don't go back.

Many people will tell you to hush if you talk about the temporariness of life.

I won't tell you to hush.

The inevitability of death can give people a reason to live. Knowing whether it goes well, or badly, it'll all come to an end one day.

It can bring us a feeling that nothing matters, which again, is another taboo.

But the beauty in this belief is if nothing matters, you can choose which life brings you the most joy. You stop worrying about the small insignificant things. You drown out the noise of everyone else's drama and opinions. Because it's all temporary.

Temporary can mean meaningful. Temporary can mean a beautiful life lived intentionally.

Detachment doesn't mean void of emotion like many new age spirituality passages will attempt to teach.

Detachment means knowing if something wants to leave, you'll let it go. Even if it causes pain and longing.

Detachment is not so much avoiding pain altogether, it's accepting temporary pain to avoid long-term suffering.

We're pack animals, attachment is our survival instinct.

There's nothing wrong with you if you find it hard to detach. But the art of knowing when to detach from people, places and situations will set you free.

Stop taking advice from people that don't inspire you. From people that don't have the same morals and values as you. You're dishonouring your own inner wisdom whenever you follow advice you know doesn't truly resonate with you.

Others may not appreciate how long it has taken you to heal. Or how much strength it took to stay alive. To make it through some of your darkest days. Many people may forget or neglect to notice that you've been extremely wounded. But I notice. I see you.

Don't downplay your growth and healing because there is no special award or acknowledgement you receive for it. Congratulate yourself. Honour your journey.

I know how much suffering and strength it took to make it this far, so be proud of yourself for that.

The idea of victim mentality is thrown around like an insult these days. The reality is, victim mentality is when someone believes everyone and everything is out to get them, and they refuse to take any accountability for their own healing or perspectives. Victim mentality is living in denial and projecting pain onto others. Victim mentality is constantly making yourself the centre of attention while intentionally ignoring other people's suffering. Think of a person screaming at an innocent customer service person over a minor inconvenience. A complete lack of empathy for anyone but themselves. That's a victim mentality.

If you're healing, if you're accepting what happened to you, if you're trying to change, if you listen to others, if you take accountability for your own behaviours and actions, you don't have a victim mentality. It's invalidating to say this to people trying to heal, an easy way to ignore their suffering and understandable temporary mistrust of everyone in the world.

For as long as there is inequality, traumatic events, unhealthy relationships, overworking, governments and authorities that do not care for their own people, poverty, elitism, wars, greed and over-consumerism, there will always be mental health problems.

This is why it's crucial to put our energy into healing ourselves and finding ways to manage our own lives first. Trying to change the whole world is going to prove itself to be an impossible task. You'll get burnt out at the thought of even trying. The solution is to change your inner world, this will create a knock-on effect on the world surrounding you.

If every person chose to heal, to find compassion, love, peace and fulfilment within themselves first, this would be a very different world to live in.

It doesn't matter if you've been hurt once or a million times, your pain is valid. The minimisation of pain by encouraging people to see that it could've been worse is so unhealthy. It's denial and it leads to bottling up emotions which then get projected onto others. No part of ignoring or minimising emotions is emotionally intelligent and anyone that tells you otherwise is a fool.

Emotional intelligence is being able to be honest with yourself about your feelings so you can let them pass on by. There will always be someone that has it worse off than you, but where do you draw the line? Does that mean that only one person in the world is entitled to having their suffering validated? The one that has experienced the most pain? Of course not. You're not being over-sensitive. If something hurts, it hurts. And if you listen to the people telling you it doesn't or shouldn't hurt, you'll hurt yourself even more by neglecting what needs to be felt.

If you've ever struggled with your relationship with food, I feel for you. All I have to say is you deserve to fuel your body, for no other reason than the simple fact you're human. That's all you need to be to be worthy of food, human. You don't need to punish yourself, love. The world is already harsh enough. You deserve to eat and you deserve to go to bed feeling full and satisfied. You deserve to have the energy to focus on more significant things in life. You deserve it even on the days when you feel like you don't. You wouldn't withhold food from a little child or a loved one, so please don't do it to yourself. You are human. Humans are worthy of food. Of feeling full and energised. It's a birthright.

If you get overstimulated quickly and full of inexplicable rage, I see you. It does not necessarily mean you have a life-long disorder. You may just be a sensitive person in a very stimulating world and that's okay. Take time to be alone. Sit in nature. Put your headphones on. Dim the lights. Switch off screens. Go to a quiet place. Take a deep breath. You're not broken. You feel and experience the world on a deeper level. It's a blessing and a curse. If you can find ways to accept yourself and meet your needs, it becomes more of a beautiful thing, to feel so deeply. To be so in tune with your surroundings.

Don't do it. Don't self-sabotage. Don't do it. Not when you've already come this far.

People talk about accepting the negative experiences that have happened to us but rarely ever talk about accepting positive experiences. You may have resistance there too. Learn to lean into the things you deserve, the achievements, the love, the people, and the opportunities. When you want to run, that's when you slow down, take a deep breath and lean into all the good the world has to offer you.

You mustn't forget, despite everything, it is a miracle you are alive. You are made of the same substance as stardust. You are made of love and light, even when you don't feel like it. You are a part of something greater, my love. The trivialities and dramas of everyday life will make you forget just how incredible and extraordinary you are. No matter how mediocre or mundane you or your life appears. Look up at the stars, and see how you are the universe experiencing itself. Put down the expectations and worries of your life for a little while and let yourself really comprehend this. You are nature. You are the universe. You are love. You are light.

Your body allows you to experience the world in a million different little ways. To fall in love. To taste new flavours. To laugh and to cry. To be intimate. To read books and watch your favourite movies. To travel and see the world. Your heart beats for you. You breathe all day and all night without having to think about it.

Really, your body is so much more beautiful than you give it credit for. Don't limit the capabilities of your body to conventional attractiveness. Your body is for you to experience this life. It is for no one but you. It is a vessel for something so much greater. And it is beautiful.

Sometimes, not all of the time, the impulses you have are the opposite of what you truly need.

You might have an impulse to isolate yourself, but really, you're tired of being misunderstood and need to feel connected. Something is bothering you and you need to voice how you feel.

You might have an impulse to run away from that opportunity, but really, you're scared of your own potential and need to follow this through to build confidence.

You might have an impulse to go full speed ahead, but really, there is no use in rushing a good thing, and you need to slow down so you can process this intentionally.

Sometimes you may need to take a step back and ask yourself is this impulse one that helps or hinders me?

To all the asexuals, aromantics, demisexuals and people that can only connect to others platonically. There is a place for you in this world. I see you. Your feelings are valid. You're not broken. You connect differently and there's nothing wrong with that. There are many people out there that feel the same. You're not alone.

You shouldn't have to fight for basic human rights. Whether it be your race, your status, your disability, your sexuality, your background, or your gender. Whatever it is. There is no justification for being stripped of your rights. You are human. Humans deserve human rights. There are people that have committed the most heinous of crimes that get treated with more regard than you, and you're discriminated against for things that are beyond your control. I'm sorry. You shouldn't have to fight to be heard. It's not right. It's not fair.

Some people will tell you it's unreasonable, delusional or toxic to hope for a better tomorrow. It's no more toxic and delusional than assuming the future is always going to get worse. Hope alone, has time and time again pulled people through horrific times, wars and economic downfalls. They'll tell you that you should always be grateful for the present moment. Sometimes the present moment is awful and denying that creates more resistance and resistance creates more suffering. You are allowed to acknowledge that right now you feel bad whilst simultaneously holding out for a better future. You cannot always control what misfortunes you face, but you are in the driver's seat and you can control which road you take. You can choose to do the little things every day to create a better tomorrow.

You are allowed to switch off the news and the mainstream media. You can take a step back. Just because it exists, does not mean you have to consume it 24/7. You can take a break. You can do your own research and be aware of current affairs in the world without filling your head with doom and gloom. People will get angry and call it selfish to not watch the news, but so be it. Your mental well-being is more important. There will always be something devastating going on in the world, and being hyper-aware of every single bad thing is not helping anyone. Action changes the world, not mindless consumption. You can start by healing, by having more compassion. People that get angry at others for not watching the news every day are rarely ever doing anything to change themselves or the world around them. They are hypocrites.

You're not going to want to hear this one but ask yourself why you're okay with chasing after someone that treats you poorly. In doing so, you are treating yourself with disrespect.

I'll give you room to process this one.

'Oh why bother with that it? It will take like 5 years!'
'You've been in this job / career / relationship / situation
/ place for so long now you might as well stay.'

Wanting new experiences doesn't take away from the
experiences you've had. You can value the time and
energy you spent with those things and people, and
recognise that you've outgrown them and desire to
move on. You can either be in the same situation in 5
years time or be living a completely different life. Only
you can decide. Don't let others downplay your dreams.

There is this vicious cycle of taking time off for your mental wellbeing, then falling behind on work, and then feeling mentally unwell again because of the pressure of catching up. This is why it's important to take scheduled breaks, whenever you can. To be gentle with yourself. To not overload yourself with extra unnecessary tasks. To tell people well you are struggling. To learn how to say no and set boundaries. To ask for help when you need it. I fully acknowledge you may get rejected, you may feel misunderstood. But keep pushing, keep being an advocate for yourself.

You're allowed to be a mess. You don't have to keep up this appearance of having your life together. You can be vulnerable. Anyone that shames you for being honest with how you feel, and your current state of mind, instead of holding space for you, isn't someone worth investing your energy into. Good relationships are the ones in which you can both celebrate the wins and provide acceptance and encouragement on the down days. The same applies to the relationship you have with yourself.

Yes, it's true. 'You haven't met all the people that are going to love you yet.'

But also, you haven't met all of the parts of yourself that you're going to love yet. You haven't experienced all of the sunsets that are going to light you up inside yet. You haven't read all of the books that make you feel seen yet. There are still new songs to be discovered. Movies that will secretly make you cry. Snacks to try that become your new favourite. Birthday presents you haven't opened. Nature trails to be walked and photographs to be taken. Recipes that make you fall in love with food again.

Next year you might be living in a completely different place. Or you might just find a new coffee order in your hometown that you love. We don't have to live our lives waiting for people to love us. We can live our lives in the hopes that every day we'll find new things we love about life.

Thank you, beautiful soul.

About the Author,

Chloë Jade resides in the United Kingdom and is the founder and writer behind @IntuitiveJournals on Instagram and TikTok. Chloë has spent her entire life thinking and feeling deeply, writing almost daily, but never sharing her thoughts or work. She felt intuitively called to share her writing one day on social media and quickly went viral, amassing tens of thousands of daily readers. Much of her teen and adult life has been dedicated to healing, and now having gone from living with debilitating c-PTSD to a place of inner peace, she longs to share her words of comfort, empathy and perspective with the world.

Made in the USA
Las Vegas, NV
12 February 2023

67371177R00135